THE PHILOSOPHY
OF AIKIDO

THE PHILOSOPHY
OF AIKIDO

JOHN STEVENS

KODANSHA INTERNATIONAL
Tokyo • New York • London

Published by Kodansha International Ltd., 17-14 Otowa 1-chome, Bunkyo-ku, Tokyo 112-8652, and Kodansha America, Inc.

Distributed in the United States by Kodansha America, Inc., 575 Lexington Avenue, New York, New York 10022, and in the United Kingdom and continental Europe by Kodansha Europe Ltd., 95 Aldwych, London WC2B 4JF.

First edition, 2001
1 2 3 4 5 6 7 8 9 04 03 02 01

ISBN 4-7700-2534-3

Library of Congress Cataloging-in-Publication Data

Stevens, John, 1947-
    The philosophy of aikido / John Stevens.— 1st ed.
    p. cm.
    Includes bibliographical references.
    ISBN 4770025343
    1. Aikido—Philosophy. 2. Ueshiba, Morihei, 1883-1969—Teachings. I. Title.

GV1114.35 .S765 2001
796.815'4—dc21
00-047822

CONTENTS

FOREWORD

The publication of *The Philosophy of Aikido* by Professor John Stevens is a significant event. Professor Stevens has been training in Aikido for many years and he has written this book based on his extensive experience and personal understanding. The author lives in Japan, and he has devoted himself to the study of Japanese culture, history, and religion on both the theoretical and practical levels. Such a comprehensive view of Japanese culture well qualifies him to write a book on the philosophy of Aikido.

Recently, numerous books have been published about Aikido. The special feature of this work is that it addresses the concerns and questions of the international Aikido community from a global perspective, derived from the integration of Eastern and Western ideals.

It is my sincere hope that *The Philosophy* of *Aikido* will become a valuable aid to Aikido practitioners all over the world.

Moriteru Ueshiba
Aikido Doshu

PREFACE

Aikido has been called the most philosophical of martial arts, and indeed Morihei Ueshiba (1883–1969), the founder of the "Way of Harmony," often told his disciples, "No philosophy, no Aikido." Master Ueshiba was martial artist supreme but his lifelong quest was primarily spiritual rather than martial. After a profound enlightenment experience at age forty-two, Master Ueshiba lectured his disciples constantly on the philosophy of Aikido, and also shared that profound system of thought with the many visitors—statesmen, religious leaders, educators, military officers, businesspeople, scientists, athletes, artists, actors, musicians, and married couples—who sought his sage counsel. Morihei Ueshiba's message was revolutionary but it was also rooted in classical tradition:

> From ancient times,
> Deep learning and martial valor
> Have been the two wheels of the Path;
> Through the virtue of practice
> Enlighten both body and soul.

Samurai warriors had to confront the vital matter of life and death, and they were naturally expected to be scholars and philosophers. Before becoming a philosopher, however, one must have years of training and extensive actual experience, and Morihei Ueshiba's wisdom was derived from a lifetime of hard training and penetrating reflection.

While the grand cosmology and esoteric teachings of Aikido have been set forth in the books *The Essence of Aikido* and *The Secrets of Aikido*, the current volume focuses on the more practical and perennial aspects of Aikido: how to view the world holistically, how to integrate body and spirit, and how to interact with other human beings in a harmonious way.

The philosophy outlined here is based on the teachings of Morihei

Ueshiba, instruction and inspiration received from my teacher Rinjiro Shirata (1912–93), who was one of Morihei's finest disciples, the writings of Kisshomaru Ueshiba (1912–98), Morihei's son and successor, and my own personal reflections derived from many years of Aikido training and study all over the world. The book is divided into two sections. The first section is a discourse on the philosophy of Aikido with the recorded teachings of Master Ueshiba serving as the core. The sayings have been compiled from published transcripts of Morihei Ueshiba's talks and interviews, extant tape recordings, and the vast oral literature. (All translations are my own.) The second is a visual, illustrated presentation of that philosophy in action. *The Philosophy of Aikido* is meant to be a companion volume to *The Spirit of Aikido* authored by Kisshomaru Ueshiba.[1] (In *The Spirit of Aikido*, Kisshomaru Ueshiba refers to his father as "Master Ueshiba." I have followed that custom here with this exception: when only the name "Morihei" appears it refers to Ueshiba as a young man, in his pre-master days.)

While *The Spirit of Aikido* was written, understandably, from a traditional Japanese perspective, *The Philosophy of Aikido* places the teachings of Aikido within the context of the emerging global culture. Old notions of "East" and "West" have been transcended, and it is now possible to find an Aikido *dojo*—and more importantly, Aikido ideas—in nearly every part of the world. The relevance and application of the insights of Aikido to daily life in this present world is the theme of the current volume. I have quoted widely from teachings of many different traditions to emphasize the universal appeal of Aikido ideals. This book is dedicated to all those who are drawn to a dynamic philosophy centered on harmony, peace, and spiritual strength.

John Stevens
Sendai and Honolulu, 2001

---

1. Details of Master Ueshiba's life can be found in John Stevens, *Invincible Warrior: A Pictorial Biography of Morihei Ueshiba, The Founder of Aikido* (Boston: Shambhala Publications, 1997) and *Three Budo Masters: Kano, Funakoshi, Ueshiba* (Tokyo: Kodansha International, 1995). See the bibliography for further information on *The Essence of Aikido, The Secrets of Aikido, The Spirit of Aikido*, and collections of Master Ueshiba's talks.

PART I

THEORY

Morihei Ueshiba discourses on the philosophy of Aikido to a group of trainees.

1

Essential Principles

As with any philosophical system, Aikido is defined by a set of essential principles.

First of all, Aikido stresses the importance of the "four gratitudes":

1. Gratitude toward the universe

This is gratitude for the gift of life, a very precious and difficult state of being to attain. According to Buddhist belief, the transmigrating soul is only as likely to find human life as a blind turtle in the great ocean who surfaces once every hundred years is liable to poke his head through a hole in a randomly floating log. And although the gods have better circumstances, their easy existence puts them in a stupor, and only human beings can become a Buddha—one needs a body to know the pain of samsara, practice the Dharma and to experience nirvana. Gratitude for being alive is supremely important, for it gives us hope. As Master Ueshiba said:

> Saints and sages have always revered the sacredness of heaven and earth, of mountains, rivers, trees, and grasses. They were always mindful of the great blessings of nature. They realized that it is the purpose of life to make the world continually afresh, to create each day anew. If you understand the principles of Aikido you too will be glad to be alive, and you will greet each day with great joy.

When you bow deeply to the universe, it bows back;
When you call out the name of God, it echoes inside you.

An Assiniboin Indian writer gave this account of his grandfather's private rite of gratitude:

He never neglected to give thanks early in the morning to the rising sun. He called the sun the Eye of the Great Spirit. At noon, he would stop for a few seconds to give thanks and receive a blessing. When the sun went down, he watched it reverently until it disappeared.

In the same spirit, upon arising Master Ueshiba faithfully paid his respects to the *dojo* shrine and greeted the morning sun. If he happened to walk by a shrine when he was traveling, he would stop to offer a prayer to the local deity, and whenever he came upon an especially beautiful sight he would thank the gods for offering up such a treat. Master Ueshiba would greet a cool breeze wafting through the *dojo* with these words: "Welcome, Mr. Breeze. How nice of you to come and refresh us!"

2. Gratitude toward our ancestors and predecessors

This includes being grateful toward the matriarchs and patriarchs of our own particular clan, and toward the many wonderful leaders, teachers, innovators, artists, and trailblazers who have come before us and created human culture. Even if our parents opposed or obstructed us in our quest we should still be grateful for the gift of our physical body. The great Judo master Kyuzo Mifune (1883–1965) often said:

I'm grateful to my parents for giving me such a small body. That way, I had to train twice as hard to beat those who were much bigger, and my technique became very powerful. I'm even grateful for injuries—I learned how to use expertly the parts of my body that were not injured.

3. Gratitude toward our fellow human beings

We cannot live without the support of other people. People who construct buildings, towns, and roads; people who make things function; people who grow and prepare our food; people who pay our salaries; people who love, nourish, and support us; people with whom we play, exercise, and train. Master Ueshiba once said to his students:

> I really have no students—you are my friends, and I learn from you. Because of your hard training, I have made it this far. I'm always grateful for your efforts and cooperation. By definition, Aikido means cooperating with everyone, cooperating with the gods and goddesses of every religion.

As the Fourteenth Dalai Lama has often pointed out, we should be grateful even for our enemies, since dealing with them helps make our spirit stronger:

> Tibet is now passing through the darkest period in its history. I regard it as a great honor and privilege to be the one to bring it through this ordeal. Perhaps if we can succeed we will not only save ourselves, but also set an important example for other countries on how nonviolence, patience, and reliance on the power of truth can be the most effective tools in human relations.

And Mahatma Gandhi (1869–1948) said, "The virtues of mercy, nonviolence, love, and truth in any man can be truly tested only when they are pitted against ruthlessness, violence, hate, and untruth."

4. Gratitude toward the plants and animals that sacrifice their lives for us

We exist at the expense of other beings in the plant and animal kingdoms, and must be grateful for each bite of food that we take.

The Zen monk Ryokan (1768–1831) would bow deeply and ask for Buddha's blessing whenever he passed farmers laboring away in the rice paddies, and he spent many hours in his hermitage chanting sutras on their behalf. He was famed for not wasting a crumb of food, and he regularly shared his meager fare with birds and wild animals. He composed this poem:

> Spring rains,
> Summer showers,
> A dry autumn.

May nature smile on us
And we all will share in the bounty.

In days past, Native American hunters never forgot to thank the animals that generously allowed themselves to be killed. Here is an Iglulik Eskimo prayer:

Beasts of the sea,
Come, offer yourselves up in the morning light.
Beasts of the plain,
Come, offer yourselves up in the morning light.

The prey was addressed as "friend" and addressed respectfully: "We are taking your life out of need, not greed." Some tribes conducted a Busk rite prior to harvest. People would gather in the square and settle or forgive all debts and quarrels of the preceding year to restore harmony in the community, and thus ensure that the crops would be gathered in a proper state of mind.

The four gratitudes can also be thought of in terms of four debts: (1) we are indebted to the universe for the gift of its grand design; (2) we are indebted to our ancestors for the gift of physical existence; (3) we are indebted to the wise men and women of the past for the gift of human culture; and (4) we are indebted to all sentient beings for the gift of sustenance.

Gratitude is a powerful antidote against the resentment we feel toward others and the ill will we harbor by holding grudges. (Buddha defined a wicked person as "one who is not grateful and who does not bear in mind the good rendered to him.") Grateful people avoid self-pity and refrain from complaining about their lot in life. Another aspect of gratitude is respect.

Native American people place great emphasis on the principle of respect: respect for Wakan Tanka, the Great Spirit; respect for Mother Earth; respect for fellow human beings; and respect for individual freedom. In Buddhism, there is a being known as the "Ever-Respectful Bodhisattva," whose sole practice is to bow deeply in gratitude to everyone he meets, giving each individual a full measure of respect for just being alive. We need to have respect for gods, goddesses, and buddhas, respect for physical objects, and, most of all, respect for other human beings. Respect is not simply consideration; it includes identification with, and sympathy for, another's position. As the Chinese proverb says, "A sorrow shared is halved; a joy shared is doubled."

Every philosophical system has a set of "morals" or "virtues." In Aikido, four primary virtues are held dear:

1. The virtue of courage

This is "brave action," "courageous commitment," and "valorous living." One must bravely face all the challenges that life dishes out and fight the good fight to the end. One must be brave enough to engage in self-sacrifice when necessary, and to admit mistakes and take full responsibility for those mistakes. The virtue of courage generates willpower and determined effort. In order to master any art, one must make an absolute commitment to practice. We train because it is difficult, not because it is easy. But if we train hard we will emerge triumphant: "Hard training leads to easy victory." In Aikido, we are taught to contest on the highest levels, going so far as to let an opponent strike first, and not to resort to attacks on easy targets. The person who is valorous wants to win fair and square and not at the expense of others. Master Ueshiba said:

> The victory we seek is to overcome all challenges and fight to the finish, accomplishing our goals. In Aikido, we never attack. If you strike first, to gain advantage over someone, that is proof that your training is insufficient, and it is really you who has been defeated.

Another aspect of courage is fearlessness. *Budo* masters often speak of the "gift of fearlessness: fearlessness that comes from all-embracing knowledge, fearlessness that comes from the destruction of illusion, fearlessness that comes from the removal of doubts, fearlessness that comes from the true understanding of the nature of pain, and fearlessness of death, the final enemy." Zen Buddhists state that "One who is wide awake has no fear." The gift of fearlessness is also the gift of assurance, making one intrepid, bold, even audacious.

The virtue of courage is symbolized by fire, a steady flame that cannot be extinguished.

2. The virtue of wisdom

Asian philosophers encouraged their students to develop a rich knowledge of heaven and earth by "reading ten thousand volumes and traveling ten thousand miles." A corollary to this is the injunction to "Never stop learning." Master Ueshiba has said:

> The universe is our greatest teacher. Look at the way a stream wends its way through a mountain valley, smoothly transforming itself as it flows over and around the rocks. The world's wisdom is contained in books, and by studying them, countless new techniques can be created. Study and practice, and then reflect on your progress. Aikido is the art of learning deeply, the art of knowing oneself.

This virtue is represented by heaven, a symbol of vast, all-encompassing knowledge.

3. The virtue of love

The term "philosophy" means "love of wisdom" and was not originally meant to describe abstract systems of thought. Pythagoras (ca. sixth century B.C.), the father of Western philosophy, defined a philosopher as one who observes, reveres, and contemplates the order, beauty, and purpose of what occurs, and looks for the golden unifying thread of essential wisdom that ties everything to together. When Pythagoras was asked, "Are you wise?" his reply was, "No, but I'm a lover of wisdom."

Love should be directed toward both objects and ideas. The Taoist philosopher, alchemist, and physician Ko Hung (ca. 284–364) said that the secret of immortality was "to extend love to all things, to the very frontiers of the universe, and to view all others as we view ourselves."

Master Ueshiba has said of love:

> In real *budo* there are no enemies. Real *budo* is the function of love. The Way of a Warrior is not to destroy and kill but to foster life, to continually create. Love is the divinity that can really protect us. Without love nothing can flourish. If there is no love between human beings, that will be the end of our world. Love generates the heat and light that sustain the world.

In Aikido philosophy, "heat" is a symbol for compassion and "light" stands for "wisdom." Earth symbolizes the warm, concrete reality of love.

Gandhi has said, "The sword of a warrior for peace is love, and the unshakable firmness that comes with it."

4. The virtue of empathy

This is the social dimension of Aikido. Philosophy can never exist in a vacuum, and we must always ask ourselves, "How do our actions affect the world in general and others in particular?" If the insights of Aikido are not applied to the realms of human relations, ecology, economy, and politics, they are of little value. Master Ueshiba said:

> First of all, you must put your own life in order. Then you must learn how to maintain ideal relations within your own family. After that, you must strive to improve conditions in your own country and finally to live harmoniously with the world at large.

Mother Teresa (1910–98) said of her works of mercy: "We do no great things, only small things with great love." When asked how to best improve the world situation, she said simply, "Greet everyone with a smile." The virtue of empathy is symbolized by water, the element that constantly nourishes the world.

(By way of comparison, the cardinal virtues of Greek philosophy are justice, prudence, fortitude, and temperance. Taoist virtues are compassion, frugality, and modesty. The Buddhist virtues are generosity, discipline, perseverance, wisdom, patience, meditation, adaptability, strength, friendliness, and equanimity. Tantric virtues include love, compassion, joy in the success of others, and equanimity toward sentient beings. Gnostic virtues are amity, reciprocity, affection, and sympathy. The virtues of a Sufi are sincerity to God, severity to self, justice to all people, service to elders, kindness to the young, generosity to the poor, good counsel to friends, forbearance with enemies, indifference to fools, and respect for the learned. The primary virtues of the Native American tribes are unselfishness, patience, and forgiveness; and the Christian virtues are faith, hope, and charity.)

The "four virtues" of Aikido help us deal with the "four challenges": old age, disease, death, and being separated from the ones we love. Life is not perfect, it is not fair, and we all suffer as a result of aging, getting sick, dying, and, worst of all, losing loved ones. This is a universal, and constant. Master Ueshiba himself had a difficult life: he faced oblivion on the battlefield during the Russo-Japanese War, and later in hand-to-hand combat with bandits in Manchuria; he lost two of his children to disease within six months of each other; he was threatened with arrest by the military government for associating with the pacifist Omoto-kyo sect; many of his friends and favorite disciples died in World War II; he saw his country vanquished and destroyed by war despite his own efforts to prevent it; he fell deathly ill at several points in his life; and he grew old (but not frail) before he finally succumbed to cancer. Master Ueshiba said:

> Each day of human life contains joy and anger, pain and pleasure, darkness and light, growth and decay. Each moment is etched with nature's grand design—do not deny or oppose the cosmic order of things. Joyfully look forward to each day and accept whatever it brings.

Life is always a trial, and all of us are subject to the wheel of fortune: an eternal round of good and bad luck, prosperity and poverty, health and illness, stability and change. By encouraging us to be braver, wiser, more loving, and more empathetic, Aikido philosophy equips us to meet painful and daunting challenges.

> Do not look upon this world with fear and loathing.
> Bravely face whatever the gods offer.

> In extreme situations, the entire universe becomes our foe; at such critical times, unity of mind and technique is essential—do not let your heart waver!

Aikido ethics revolve around one principle: *makoto*. The literal meaning of *makoto* is "true acts," and the word denotes "sincerity that is natural, spontaneous—free of duplicity and artifice." Human beings are essentially good, in the Aikido view—they are naturally pure, bright, honest, and gentle. George Catlin (1796–1872), who spent time with nearly fifty Indian tribes, wrote, "I love a people who keep the commandments without ever having read them or heard them preached." Such natural observance of the commandments is *makoto*. Good consists of the pleasant things in life; evil is that which causes unhappiness, misfortune, disharmony.

Master Ueshiba emphasized the three philosophical principles of unity:

1. Your mind should be in harmony with the functioning of the universe.
2. Your body should be in tune with the movement of the universe.
3. Body and mind should be as one, unified with the activity of the universe.

In other words, one should never do anything that is contrary to nature. If your practice were *makoto*, you would not be opposed to nature in the first place, but most of us have to rely on *nen*, or "concentrated focus on ideal principles," to remain attuned on all levels.

The physical form of the Aikido techniques is nothing special. Master Ueshiba studied many different kinds of martial arts, and incorporated a variety of techniques into his system. Many of the movements are found in the martial arts of the Western world, such as wrestling and fencing. The techniques are physical vehicles employed to reach a higher level of understanding. Master Ueshiba said:

> The techniques of Aikido change constantly; every encounter is unique, and the appropriate response should emerge naturally. Today's techniques will be different tomorrow. Do not get caught up with form and appearance. Ultimately, you must forget about technique.

Aikido techniques are vehicles of transformation, with four aspects: educational, historical, practical, and philosophical. The techniques are supported by nine pillars, which can also be interpreted as nine philosophical gates of wisdom with wide applicability. The nine pillars are:

1. Shiho, "universality"
The literal meaning of *shiho* is "four-directions." In Classical Aikido, prac-

tice begins with *shiho-giri*, "four-directions cut," which symbolizes the four gratitudes, the four virtues, and the four challenges. *Shiho* also means to look at the world in all its aspects, to consider things from all angles, and to be able to move in any direction as necessary. Symbolically, the four directions represent different virtues: the east is knowledge; the south, growth; the west, liberation; and the north, strength.

2. Irimi, *"entering and blending"*

When confronted with an attack in Aikido, a typical response is not to retreat or to deflect the aggression but to enter right into the face of the attack: "When an opponent comes forward, move in and greet him." Sometimes we end up facing the same direction as the attacker, in close proximity—so close that it is difficult to discern the difference between attacker and defender. Often the best way to deal with opposition is to go right to its source, and then blend with it, rendering further aggression impossible.

3. Kaiten, *"opening and turning"*

Sometimes it is better to avoid an attack by opening to the side and then redirecting the attack toward the aggressor. The concept of "opening" is central in Aikido, and encompasses being open to possibility, open-minded, and openhearted. Master Ueshiba said:

> Each one of us has to open our own path, to open our own door to truth. The universe is like an open book that can be read, and we should look at the world as it really is.

There is a Hasidic saying that "God is everywhere he is allowed to enter. He is in our hearts if we do not shut him out." Some fervent Hasids walk around with their chests exposed as a sign that their heart is always "open" to God.

The word "universe" literally means "one turn"; the universe turns all around and within us—we are, in a fundamental sense, the pivot of the world. We have a saying, "turn one's life around" (to make thing better), and this coincides with another important aspect of *kaiten*. Master Ueshiba told his students, "The secret of *kaiten* movements lies in your mind, not your body."

4. Kokyu, "breath power and good timing"
Breath is life, and troubled breathing is usually a sign of stress, sickness, or fear. There are a number of exercises in Aikido that teach us how to foster deep and powerful breathing by tapping into the all-pervading breath of the universe (one exercise is given in the chapter, "Aikido and Tantra"). Master Ueshiba has said:

> Everything in heaven and earth breathes. Breath is the thread that ties creation together. When the myriad variations in universal breath can be sensed, the individual techniques of Aikido are born.

Many of Master Ueshiba's students remarked that they could execute the techniques well enough when he was in the *dojo* with them, but that as soon as he was gone, they started to have difficulty. "That is because," Master Ueshiba explained, "when I am present I link our *kokyu* together and we function as one."

Another meaning of *kokyu* is "good timing." This involves understanding the rhythms of life, and being in tune with one's surroundings and circumstances.

5. Osae, "self-control and control of a situation"
Aikido techniques include a number of pins and locks used to control an attack. The underlying implication of such locks and pins is that one should "keep a firm grip on the matter," "keep a situation under control before it gets out of hand," and "put a lid on things when they flare up." As it says in the *Tao Te Ching*, "Tackle things before they appear: cultivate peace and order to suppress chaos."

6. Ushiro-waza, "dealing with the unknown"
In Aikido, we practice being attacked from the rear in order to foster a sixth sense that perceives aggression before it occurs. In daily life this translates into the idea of "expecting the unexpected," especially from those misguided souls who try to stab us in the back or blindside us.

7. Tenchi, "standing firmly between heaven and earth"

Our universe is composed of heaven (emptiness), earth (form), and human beings (a combination of both elements). Our lives unfold in conjunction with the movements of heaven and earth, and we should try to maintain our equilibrium between those two polarities. Master Ueshiba has said:

> Always try to remain in communion with heaven and earth; then the universe will appear in its true light. If you perceive the true form of heaven and earth, you will be enlightened to your own true form.

8. Aiki ken and aiki jo, "the sword of resolution and the staff of intuition"

In Aikido, the techniques are defined by the straight, direct, and true movements of the sword. To be successful in life too, we must act resolutely, singlemindedly, and honestly. However, we also need good intuition to know when to avoid an attack. For that we must be able to act as flexibly as does the shaft in Aikido stick movements; it shifts smoothly up and down and to the right and left, depending on the circumstances.

9. Ukemi, "seven times down, eight times up"

One of the first things an Aikido student learns is *ukemi*, "breakfalls" that allow him or her to take a safe fall and spring back up. The vicissitudes of life will similarly bring us down with heavy blows, but we need to get back up each time. *Ukemi* also means to bounce back from a mistake. As Master Ueshiba said: "Failure is the key to success; each mistake teaches a valuable lesson." *Ukemi* can also be thought of as a kind of "prostration," an exercise in humility, determination, and security—which indicates that you are not too proud to be thrown, and that you are determined to get up again.

Another key principle of Aikido philosophy is *muteiko*, or "nonresistance."

> Aikido is the principle of nonresistance. That which is nonresistant is victorious from the beginning. Those with evil intentions or contentious thoughts are instantly vanquished. A true warrior is invincible because he or she contests nothing.

Muteiko is very similar to the Taoist notion of *wu wei*, "nonaction" or "nonassertion." The *Tao Te Ching* states:

A good soldier is not martial.
A good fighter does not get angry.
The best way to conquer an enemy is not to engage him.

By not impeding the natural flow of things and not attempting to interfere in the unfolding of events, we achieve harmony with our environment. There is a well-known tale about a Taoist butcher whose knife never went dull because his blade found the empty spaces between the joints and the ox just fell apart. When performed by a master, Aikido techniques look similarly effortless, and this is *wu wei*—subtle, still movements that are incomparably sharp and powerful.

Another possible translation of *muteiko* is "nonviolence," or *ahimsa* in the Sanskrit. Like Gandhi, Master Ueshiba believed that the source of all evil is violence: violence toward oneself, toward others, or toward the environment: "To smash, injure, or destroy is the worst sin that a human being can commit." (In her Nobel Peace Prize acceptance speech, Mother Teresa lamented our world's pervasive violence toward the unborn: "The greatest destroyer of peace is abortion. If a mother can kill her own child, what is left?")

Gandhi did not like *ahimsa* to be translated as "passive resistance" because he felt that this would lend the word an unfortunate connotation of weakness or powerlessness. He preferred the term "nonviolence"—a much more positive concept. Since Gandhi was preaching to Hindus, who already had a tradition of *ahimsa*, he sometimes said that the nonviolence of Muslim leader Abdul Hamid Khan (1880–1976) was far superior to his own, because Khan was "teaching nonviolence to people who have always been armed to the teeth." One of Gandhi's top disciples, Vinoba Bhave (1895– 1982), never verbally opposed his chief adversaries—rich landlords whom he was trying to persuade to donate land to the homeless. Bhave felt that opposition itself was a form of violence, because opposition creates insecurity and often makes a person more intransigent. "Whenever I deal with a greedy landlord," Bhave said of his *ahimsa* strategy, "I do not argue but instead try to find a door to his heart that will convince him."

Martin Luther King (1929–68), another advocate of nonviolence, stated,

All life is interrelated, all humanity is involved in a single process, and to the degree I harm my brother, to that extent I am harming myself.

Similarly, Master Ueshiba said:

As soon as you concern yourself with the "good" and "bad" of your fellows, you create an opening in your heart for maliciousness to enter. Testing, competing with, and criticizing others weakens and defeats you.

In Christian terms, we have this saying of Jesus's:

You have heard that it was said, "An eye for an eye and a tooth for a tooth." But I say to you, Do not resist an evildoer. But if anyone strikes you on the right cheek, turn the other also. (Matthew 6: 38–39)

The idea of "turning the other cheek" is represented in Aikido philosophy by the term *kaiten*, "to turn the attack around and let it go by."

Another ingenious use of nonviolence is described in the play *Lysistrata* by Aristophanes (ca. 448–385 B.C.). Lysistrata planned to stop the war between Athens and Sparta by getting the women of Greece to refuse sex with the men until the conflict ended. When Lampito the Spartan heard of this plan he said, "It will probably work. They say that Menelaus threw away his sword when he saw Helen of Troy's breasts."

The last major principle of Aikido philosophy is *masakatsu agatsu katsu hayabi*. The character *masa* means "true, correct, straight," while *katsu* is "victory, triumph, success." The Dalai Lama described the term *masakatsu*, or "True Victory," this way:

Ours is a civilization that for a thousand years has been dedicated to nonviolence, compassion, and forgiveness, and therefore we struggle for our rights as a people within the parameters of these principles. If we were to abandon them and regain our land through hatred and violent means the loss would far outweigh the gain. The Tibet that we would get back would no longer be the Tibet for which we are struggling. We would have an outer victory, but an inner defeat.

Here are some other examples of *masakatsu*:
When he was a lawyer, Abraham Lincoln (1809–65) told his colleagues:

> Persuade your neighbors to compromise whenever you can. Point out to them how the nominal winner is often a real loser—in fees, expenses, and waste of time. As a peacemaker the lawyer has a superior opportunity of being a good man.

The *Dhammapada* states,

> "He reviled me, he beat me, he defeated me, he deprived me." In those who harbor such grudges, hatred never ceases.

> Hatred never ceases by hatred at any time. Hatred ceases by love; this is an eternal truth.

The *Tao Te Ching* says:

> If you attack with compassion, you will win.
> If you defend with compassion, you will stand firm.

And another Taoist verse states:

> To the mind that is still
> The whole world surrenders.

Masakatsu can be interpreted as meaning: "If your work is true, it will emerge victorious and endure." Reliance upon this aspect of *masakatsu* is valuable when dealing with criticism. Many Islamic scholars wrote theological and legal opinions against Sufi Master Rumi's (ca. 1201–70) innovative use of music and dancing in his school. But "out of kindness and generous understanding"—in other words, maintaining an attitude of *masakatsu*—Rumi made no reply to his critics. Objections diminished, and now his critics and their opinions are totally forgotten.

Master Ueshiba once defined *masakatsu* as "accomplishing your purpose on earth."

A is "oneself" and *gatsu* (*katsu*) is "victory." This is "self-victory," a triumph over one's inner demons, one's base instincts. Aikido is an occasion not for correcting others, it is for correcting yourself. Master Ueshiba said:

> Aikido begins with you. Work on yourself and your appointed task. Everyone has a spirit that can be refined, a body that can be trained in some manner, a suitable path to follow. Foster peace in your own life and apply Aikido to all that you encounter.

Haya means "swift, quick, dynamic," while *bi* (*hi*) is "sun, day, light, time." *Katsu hayabi* is "victory swift and immediate." A close translation of the entire phrase, *masakatsu agatsu katsu hayabi*, would be: "True victory is victory over oneself, right here, right now!" *Masakatsu agatsu katsu hayabi* was Master Ueshiba's most frequent reply to the question, "What is Aikido?"

On the level of practice, *masakatsu agatsu katsu hayabi* can be interpreted as,

> Unflinching courage
> coupled with unflagging effort
> until all aims are suddenly accomplished.

In technical terms, the phrase says:

> If your mind is clear
> and your movements true,
> the technique immediately manifests itself.

In terms of its more inward, philosophical meaning, the phrase suggests,
> You will emerge victorious
> By subduing your lower nature
> And realizing a state of being that transcends time and space.

At the stage of liberation, the words indicate that:

> The truth will free you from fear
> and self-doubt,
> and each and every moment will appear vital and bright.

2

Aikido, Nature, and Health

Morihei Ueshiba was a child of nature. Until moving to Tokyo in his late for-
ties, he spent most of his life outdoors: as a young man residing in Wakayama
Prefecture, he fished and swam in the ocean, worked in the fields, trained in
the woods, and traversed the sacred mountains of Kumano to visit temples and
shrines; as a pioneer in the wilds of Hokkaido in his thirties, he was a full-time
farmer and logger; and in the years just before his move to Tokyo, he was in
charge of the extensive organic gardens at the Omoto-kyo compound in Aya-
be. In Wakayama, Hokkaido, and Iwama alike, Master Ueshiba practiced ritual
purification in the icy ocean, under waterfalls, and in rapidly flowing streams.

Master Ueshiba's enlightenment experience occurred in a garden:

> Suddenly the earth trembled. Golden vapor welled up from the
> ground and engulfed me. I felt transformed into a golden image,
> and my body seemed as light as a feather. All at once I under-
> stood the nature of creation: the way of a warrior is to manifest
> divine love, a spirit that embraces and nurtures all things. Tears of
> gratitude streamed down my cheeks. I saw the entire earth as my
> home, and the sun, moon, and stars as my intimate companions.

Interestingly, Hildegard of Bingen (1098–1179), one of the great female
mystics of the West, was also aged forty-two when she was transformed by a
similar blast of light:

A burning light of tremendous brightness coming from heaven poured into my entire mind. Like a flame that does not burn but enkindles, it inflamed my whole heart and my entire breast, just like the sun that warms an object with its rays. Thereafter I was able to understand the hidden meaning of all the books of the Bible.

In Shinto mysticism, it is believed that advanced adepts such as Master Ueshiba on occasion enter a state beyond time and space and become one with the divine. This transcendent experience is said to be accompanied by a blast of light, typically golden, but sometimes purple. This is the source of Master Ueshiba's statement that "The universe turned into purple smoke and entered my body."

Master Ueshiba was never really at home in the metropolis of Tokyo. He acquired farmland in Iwama in rural Ibaraki Prefecture, where he built an outdoor *dojo* and then spent as much time there as possible. No matter where he was, Master Ueshiba was on hand to greet the morning sun, and usually recited his Shinto prayers outdoors, rather than inside a building.

> Create each day anew by clothing yourself with heaven and earth, bathing yourself with wisdom and love, and placing yourself in the heart of Mother Nature.

The Hasidic saint Baal Shem Tov (ca. 1700–60) taught his followers:

> The world is new to us every morning—this is God's gift to us, and we should believe that we are reborn every day.

Master Ueshiba viewed nature as our primary and most inspiring teacher, and his philosophy was rooted in the natural world:

> Consider the ebb and flow of the tide. When the waves come to strike the shore, they crest and fall, creating a sound. Your breath should follow the same pattern, absorbing the universe in your belly with each inhalation. Know that we all have access to four treasures: the energy of the sun and moon, the breath of heaven, the breath of earth, and the ebb and flow of the tide.

> Study the teachings of the pine tree, the bamboo, and the plum blossom. The pine is evergreen, firmly rooted, and venerable.

The bamboo is strong, resilient, unbreakable. The plum blossom is hardy, fragrant, and elegant.

Your heart is full of fertile seed, waiting to sprout. Just as a lotus flower springs from the mire to bloom splendidly, the interaction of the cosmic breath causes the flower of the spirit to bloom and bear fruit in this world.

Those who practice Aikido must protect the domain of Mother Nature, the divine reflection of creation, and keep it lovely and fresh. The subtle techniques of Aikido arise as naturally as the appearance of spring, summer, autumn, and winter.

Spring forth from the Great Earth;
Billow like Great Waves;
Stand like a tree, sit like a rock;
Use the One to strike All.
Learn and forget!

In the West, there is this saying of Saint Bernard of Clairvaux (1090–1153): "Trees and stones will teach you that which you can never learn from books."

The two *kanji* characters that comprise the word *aiki* are *ai*, meaning "to come together, to blend, to join" and *ki*, "life force, spirit, disposition." The tendency of matter to cohere is a basic fact of the universe. There are chemical bonds, nuclear bonds, and human bonds that fuse with an intense energy. Master Ueshiba defined *aiki* as:

The life force that brings all things together; it is the optimal process of unification that operates in all realms, from the vastness of space to the tiniest atoms.

When he first started teaching, Master Ueshiba called his art "*Aioi-jutsu*." *Aioi* means "mutually arising," and it is described in the *Tao Te Ching* like this:

Being and non-being are mutually arising.
Difficult and easy complement each other.
Long and short exhibit each other.
High and low measure each other.

Sound and voice harmonize each other.
Front and back follow each other.

Aioi-jutsu formed the basis of Aikido.

Do, the third character in the word *ai-ki-do*, means "Path" or "Way," and is the same character used by Taoists to describe the mysteries of nature. Late in life, Master Ueshiba in fact looked much more like a benign Taoist immortal than a fierce warrior, and he described *do* as:

> The Way is like the veins that circulate blood through our bodies, following the natural flow of the life force. If you are separated in the slightest from that divine essence, you are far off the path.

Master Ueshiba also compared the Way with water, which always seeks the best course, flowing around obstacles, offering no resistance.

Taoists (the Way), Buddhists (the Eightfold Path of right views, right intentions, right speech, right action, right livelihood, right effort, right mindfulness, and right concentration), Christians ("I am the Way" John 14: 6), and Muslims (the Straight Path) often speak of a Path or Way, and they all agree that it is easy to get lost or be seduced by apparent shortcuts. Singleminded effort is always needed to traverse the Way because the beginning is sure to be bumpy and hard to follow. Master Ueshiba has said:

> Lose your way
> And you will
> Enter a bad path;
> Do not give rein to the
> Wild stallion of your heart.

The further one progresses, though, the more the road grows smoother and wondrous sights appear along the way.

> Aiki—
> A Path so difficult
> To comprehend,
> Yet as simple as
> The natural flow of Heaven.

Ultimately, each one of us has our own path:

Many paths lead to the peak of Mount Fuji, but the goal is the same. There are many methods of reaching the top, but all can bring us to the heights. There is no need to battle with each other —we are all brothers and sisters who should walk the path together.

And it is the individual walking on the path—the actual practice of Aikido —that is important, rather than the path itself.

Rebbe Yaakov-Yitzhak of Lubin (d. 1815) said:

There are many paths leading to perfection; it is up to us to choose our own path, and follow it with great determination, to make it our own truth.

Before he died, Rebbe Zusia (d. 1800) said to his disciples:

When I come before the heavenly tribunal, I will not be asked why I was not Abraham, Jacob, or Moses. I will be asked why I was not Zusia.

Nature, in the Aikido scheme of things, functions according to the principle of "one spirit, four souls, three fundamentals, eight powers" (*ichirei-shikon-sangen-hachiriki*).

Almost every cosmology, East or West, posits a first cause, a single source, or a big bang from which the universe came into being. Master Ueshiba explained Aikido creation in terms of the cosmic seed syllable SU:

There was no heaven, no earth, no universe, just empty space. In this vast emptiness, a single point suddenly manifested itself. From that point, steam, smoke, and mist spiraled forth in a luminous sphere and the *kototama* SU was born. As SU expanded circularly up and down, left and right, nature and breath began, clear and uncontaminated. Breath developed life, and sound appeared. SU is the "Word" mentioned in the Christian Bible.

In Sufi philosophy, this seed syllable is HU, the name of the most high, and the origin of all sounds and, by extension, of all activity.

Master Ueshiba also referred to SU as the One Spirit.

All things, material and spiritual, originate from One Spirit and are related as if they are one family. There is evil and disorder in this world because people have forgotten One Spirit.

Master Ueshiba often spoke of "one family, one generation, one world, one body, one year, one day" emanating from the One Spirit. The *Isha Upanishad* declares: "He who sees everywhere the Oneness will be free of grief and delusion." The Taoists say, "Hold on to the Center to realize the Oneness of Heaven and Earth." From One Spirit creation emerged, based on the interaction of fire and water.

In the East and West alike, fire and water are seen as the two principal forces of creation. In Asian cosmology, fire and water arise from the Great One: fire flames and rises, water moistens and flows down. From the interaction of fire and water, all things are engendered. In order to live, we need water to drink, and fire to cook our food. In Western alchemy, fire provides form and water provides matter, thus creating the "pure gold" of existence. Fire and water are the source of life, but both need to be respected and handled properly, since they can destroy as well as nourish. Alcohol, for example, is sometimes called "firewater." Used properly it is an elixir of vital energy; used to excess it becomes a deadly poison. Within the human body, the fire element is centered around the heart; the water element is associated with the kidneys. Symbolically, in alchemy, fire consumes and water purifies. Master Ueshiba said, "All Aikido techniques originate from the subtle interaction of fire and water."

In physical terms, the four souls are heaven, fire, water, and earth. In the West, the order of the four elements is formulated a bit differently, as fire, air (= heaven), water, and earth. In Aikido philosophy, the extension of heaven and earth, and the interaction of fire and water between those two poles is emphasized while Greek philosophy groups the "lighter" and "heavier" elements together. Modern physics postulates the four elements as gravity, electromagnetic force, weak nuclear force, and strong nuclear force. In spiritual and psychological terms, the four souls of Aikido philosophy describe different aspects of human nature:

1. *Kushi-mitama* ("wonderful soul") is the intelligent, profound, mysterious, and sensitive aspect of human nature. It is the

source of wisdom, clarity, and virtue. In the human body, *kushi-mitama* functions through the nervous system.

2. *Ara-mitama* ("wild soul") is the rough, wild, and fierce aspect of human nature. It is the source of courage, valor, and industry, but if it is not controlled and properly channeled, it can be destructive. In the body, *ara-mitama* functions through the bones, muscles, and internal organs.

3. *Nigi-mitama* ("pacific soul") is the peaceful, gentle, and mild aspect of human nature. It is the source of empathy, trust, respect and friendship. In the body, *nigi-mitama* functions through the blood, skin, brain, sense organs, and lymph glands.

4. *Sachi-* (or *saki-*) *mitama* ("happy soul") is the optimistic, bright, and flourishing aspect of the human soul. It is the source of love and compassion. In the body, *sachi-mitama* functions through the hormones.

Originally, *ara-mitama* and *nigi-mitama* were considered primary. The *ara-mitama* was needed to summon up the courage to defend one's space, physical and psychological, while the *nigi-mitama* was required to restore peace and harmony once a threat had passed. *Sachi-mitama* and *kushi-mitama* were said to have evolved from *nigi-mitama*. In Aikido philosophy, however, the four souls are grouped together, and the most subtle soul, the *kushi-mitama*, is placed first, in keeping with the priority that Aikido places on the innate goodness of human nature.

The four souls are somewhat akin to the four cardinal humors of Western medieval thought, which were thought to determine one's disposition and health: sanguine (warm, passionate, and cheerful); phlegmatic (in its positive sense, meaning calm and composed; in its negative sense, sluggish and apathetic); choleric (quick-tempered and irascible); and melancholy (sad, gloomy, and depressed). But while three of the Western humors are essentially negative, all of the four souls are essentially positive, with only the *ara-mitama* a possible troublemaker. However, each of the four souls can become warped and produce its opposite: mad soul, fighting soul, evil soul, contentious soul.

There are two other aspects to the human soul of which Master Ueshiba often spoke: "conscious soul" (*kon*) and "corporeal soul" (*haku*). (In the

Kabbala, these two entities are known as *neshamah* and *nefesh*.) The conscious soul represents the higher nature of a human being; intelligence, conscience, spiritual sensitivity, and intuition. The corporeal soul is baser in nature, the seat of emotions: joy, sadness, anger, fear, love, hate, and desire. An admixture of conscious soul and corporeal soul is necessary for human existence —pure soul would have no body—but Aikido philosophy emphasizes the development of the conscious soul: "Vitalize, animate, and nourish the conscious aspect of your soul, and you will naturally become more spiritual."

One of Master Ueshiba's key messages was that the old martial arts were primarily base in nature, centered on fear, aggression, conquest, and brute force. Aikido, however, stresses fearlessness, harmonization, peace, and spiritual strength; it is the enlightened warrior ethic of the New Age.

In Aikido philosophy, nature also has "four dimensions": diamond, willow, flowing, and *ki*. Modern physics describes these four as: solid, liquid, gaseous, and plasma (the stuff of the sun and stars). In human terms, the four are: diamond (hard bones); willow (soft flesh); flowing (circulation of blood); and *ki* (breath). Technically, one should be, depending on the circumstances, hard as a diamond, flexible as a willow, smooth-flowing like water, or as indiscernible but pervasive as breath.

Ki (*ch'i* in Chinese) is the life force, the energy field that sustains the world. *Ki* is not easy to define—even great Chinese sages such as Mencius (ca. 380–289 B.C.) admitted that the concept defied precise explanation: "It is not a 'what,' it is unnamable" was a typical nonspecific description—but here are some possibilities: "spirit," "breath," "vital energy," "vivifying force," "cosmic energy," "ethereal essence." *Ki* has also been likened to *prana* (Indian philosophy), *pneuma* (Greek), and *ruah* (Kabbalah).

On an individual level, *ki* functions as breath, energy, and the human aura. On the cosmic level, *ki* is manifest as air, steam, and vital force. Ko Hung stated that a human being is within the ever-changing flow of cosmic *ki* while at the same time possessing his or her own internal ocean of *ki*. The goal of both Taoist and Aikido practice is to link the two kinds of *ki*.

Here I would like to relate a personal experience of the interaction between individual and cosmic *ki*.

During my training in Japan, I spent a long period, lasting several years, sitting regularly in early-morning meditation outdoors under the eaves of an old temple. The style was supposed to be Zen meditation, but it soon became much more of a Taoist/Aikido practice. I felt immersed in nature, breathing with the cosmos, and linked intimately to the *ki* environment around me. The year in Japan is traditionally divided into twenty-four *ki* periods and I experienced them all, gradually learning to sense (and appreciate) the subtle changes that each day brought. I came to understand the Zen saying:

> I sit quietly doing nothing.
> Spring comes, grass grows of itself.

The twenty-four *ki* periods are:

1. Winter solstice	22 December
2. Lesser cold	6 January
3. Great cold	20 January
4. Beginning of spring	4 February
5. Rain waters	19 February
6. Awakening of creatures from hibernation	6 March
7. Spring equinox	21 March
8. Clear brightness	5 April
9. Great rain	21 April
10. Beginning of summer	6 May
11. Lesser fullness of grain	22 May
12. Grain in ear	6 June
13. Summer solstice	22 June
14. Lesser heat	8 July
15. Great heat	23 July
16. Beginning of autumn	2 August
17. End of heat	24 August
18. White dew	8 September
19. Autumn equinox	23 September
20. Cold dew	9 October
21. Descent of hoar frost	24 October
22. Beginning of winter	8 November
23. Lesser snow	23 November
24. Greater snow	8 December

Much later I spent six months in Hawaii, where I swam in the ocean every day. In Hawaii the seasonal changes are not so dramatic—in fact, most people, including me at first, don't think there are any changes at all—but each day at the beach was distinctly different—the temperature, the tide, the waves, the breeze, the color of the water, the refraction of the sunlight, the density of the drifting clouds. This nature meditation was more active and the *ki* energy far more direct and powerful but here, too, I sometimes ceased to exist and started to be.

Master Ueshiba made a distinction between two forms of *ki*:

> There are two types of *ki*: ordinary *ki* and true *ki*. Ordinary *ki* is coarse and heavy: true *ki* is light and versatile. In order to perform well, you have to liberate yourself from ordinary *ki* and permeate your organs with true *ki*. Strength resides where one's *ki* is concentrated and stable; confusion and maliciousness arise when *ki* stagnates.

Technically, *aiki* is used to harmonize oneself, both mentally and physically, with an attack, since attacks occur on both mental and physical levels (with an intention to attack preceding the act itself). In Aikido we train to sense aggression and then to redirect the actual attack through one of the nine pillars mentioned in Chapter 1. Off the mat too we try to be aware of possible conflicts and, if something does come up, we try to neutralize it—usually verbally, but also by body language and general attitude. In the *dojo*, we stress a straight, balanced *ki*-filled posture that leans neither to the right nor the left. In daily life, this would be a centered attitude that avoids bias.

If the two characters are reversed we have *kiai*, a state so full of *ki* that it has to be expressed as a vigorous shout. Adepts like Master Ueshiba can actually knock people down with their *kiai*. There is a very interesting passage regarding the use of *kiai* by Jesus (John 18: 3–6). A band of soldiers accompanied by a group of chief priests and Pharisees came to arrest Jesus. He said to them "Whom do you seek?" They replied, "Jesus of Nazareth." When Jesus replied, "I am he!" his *kiai* knocked them backward and they fell to the ground in a heap. In an earlier incident (Luke 4: 30), Jesus had miraculously escaped from a lynch mob so these two incidents meant that he could have escaped, using Aikido principles, if he had wanted to; indeed,

Jesus voluntarily surrendered to the startled soldiers when they got up, telling Peter, "Am I not to drink from the cup my father has given me?" ("I am he" can also be interpreted as "Here I am!" This latter was the expression used by Abraham and Moses when they spoke to God.)

While we usually associate *kiai* with deafening shouts, *kiai* can be silent but just as powerful. My Japanese calligraphy teacher was a tiny woman, half my size, and not particularly robust physically since she had been having an on-and-off battle with breast cancer. However, her soundless *kiai*—"energy fully manifest"—was so powerful that she could immobilize my hand with the slightest touch, to prevent me from going the wrong way when she helped me trace out the brushstrokes. (She was also continually surprising me by looking at my brushwork and making right-on-the-money comments like "Are you hungry?" or "Did you get some good news?")

The Three Fundamentals are the building blocks of the universe: triangle, circle, square. The triangle represents the generation of energy and is the most stable physical posture. It represents the different trinities that shape our universe, including:

> heaven, earth, humankind
> body, mind, spirit
> being, consciousness, bliss
> man, woman, child
> birth, life, death
> truth, goodness, beauty
> animal, vegetable, mineral
> past, present, future
> Brahma, Vishnu, Shiva
> Sarasvati, Lakshmi, Kali
> Ame no Minaka Nushi, Takami Musubi no Kami, Kami Musubi
>   no Kami

(The last triad is that of the Shinto deities of creation. The long names with similar sounds are a bit daunting, but in essence the three deities can be explained as center, plus, and minus. The meaning of the name of Ame no Minaka Nushi is "Lord Deity of Heaven's Center." This primal deity is both immanent and transcendent, the totality of creation, the heart of being.

Ame no Minaka Nushi is the cosmic center. Like most ultimate principles, Ame no Minaka Nushi is difficult to describe and in is fact only mentioned once in the *Kojiki*, Japan's chronicle of creation—it is simply beyond words. The "next" two gods manifest more particular aspects: Takami Musubi no Kami, "High August Growth Deity," is a (masculine) symbol of centripetal force, the fire element, and that which expands, swells, exhales, and diversifies; Kami Musubi no Kami, "Divine August Growth Deity," is a (feminine) symbol of centrifugal force, the water element, and that which contracts, absorbs, inhales, and unifies. These are all things that can be experienced by human beings and the two deities are yet another way to represent the cosmic interaction of yin and yang, fire and water, emptiness and form.)

Returning to the second of the three fundamentals, the circle symbolizes serenity and perfection, the source of unlimited techniques. It stands for the principle of flexibility and suppleness. A circle with a dot in the center represents resolution, harmony of all polarities, and continuous revolution.

The square is a symbol of solidity, the basis of applied control. It represents totality, permanence, stability, and honesty.

The eight powers are the complementary forces that give the universe body:

movement	calm
release	solidification
contraction	expansion
unification	division

In Western philosophy, the eight powers were defined as the four elements of earth, water, air, and fire crossed with the four qualities: cold (contraction), hot (expansion), wet (dissolution), and dry (crystallization).

Musubi is the procreative force that brings nature into being and holds all life—the "one spirit, four souls, three fundamentals, eight powers"—together. *Musu* means generate, produce; *bi* is "spirit, wonder, strange power." *Musubi* is the generation of wonders: the continual unification of opposites, the marvelous union of male and female. *Musubi* is the endless cycle of creation—even death is *musubi*, a link to a different, cosmic realm. In human terms, the mother (*mater*, in Latin = matter) conjoins with the father (*pater* = pattern) to give birth (*natus*). *Musubi* is the science of creation and the art of bringing things into being. Intriguingly, in modern physics there is a string theory that postulates ten dimensions (length, width, and height as three triads plus the flow of time) bound together by strings that hold the whole universe in place. Master Ueshiba once declared the purpose of Aikido to be "the tying together of everything."

In Aikido, we have the concept of *ki-musubi*. In the physical techniques, one attempts to tie up his or her *ki* with that of the partner to neutralize an attack. In daily life, *ki-musubi* can be applied to all the different aspects of existence—human relations, interaction with the environment, the acts of drinking and eating—to blend them into a unified whole. In this sense, *ki-musubi* means "integral and creative living."

Like any system of physical culture, Aikido promotes health through thorough stretching of the body, deep breathing, *ki* development, and balanced movement. It is quite possible to practice Aikido as a kind of Yoga or Chi-Kung (without the fussiness about what you can and cannot eat or, for a man, how often you can ejaculate). Master Ueshiba said:

> Aikido is good for the health. It helps you manifest your inner and outer beauty. It fosters good manners and proper deportment. When one's *ki* is circulating freely, sickness does not arise.

Master Ueshiba was naturally interested in the health of the human body. Despite his superhuman strength, he suffered from chronic indigestion and also had a weak liver, but he used his *ki* power to overcome these infirmities to a large extent. He himself loved to be massaged in the evening after a long day of training, and encouraged his followers to learn as much about the body as possible. The locks and pins in Aikido are designed to stimulate the joints, and serve as a vigorous form of massage. There is a lot of touching in Aikido, and in Oriental medicine, a "hands-on approach" is essential for healing (similar to the sentiment expressed in Christian hymns: "He touched me and made me whole.")

Kototama, or "spirit sounds," which will be discussed in detail in the next chapter, have definite healing properties. When Master Ueshiba was feeling out of sorts, which was quite often, he would intone the *kototama* SU-U-U to revive his *ki*. Mantras and other sacred sounds have always been considered a valid form of medicine in traditional societies the world over, and this function is confirmed by modern science. In an impromptu experiment in

1971 at North Middlesex Hospital in England, someone decided to treat three comatose patients (who had been in comas of sixty-three, fourteen, and thirteen days respectively) by putting earphones on them that played the BBC's Radio One programming of popular music. After two days, all the patients were speaking for the first time since their injuries. Within five days, they were all walking. This unexpected development (to modern scientists) spurred more systematic research on the healing property of sound. I have personally seen *kototama* medicine work well with desperately brain-damaged and retarded children.

It is also becoming clear to modern health professionals that their attitude —their *aiki* identification with patients—has a positive effect. Healing is a two-way process, and even with the most advanced medical technology, sympathetic human interaction can be crucial. Hippocrates (ca. 460–360 B.C.), the father of Western medicine, realized this: "There is a common flow, one common breath, and all things are in sympathy."

However, Aikido is perhaps most valuable as a system for promoting good mental health. Our most fundamental disease is ignorance, and Aikido philosophy provides us with plenty of wisdom to combat that condition. Many other illnesses are caused by an imbalance in our lives, and Aikido philosophy helps to remedy that as well. Of course, we would all like to practice under optimal conditions, but Aikido teaches us how to handle situations that are less than ideal. It goes so far as to teach us to welcome adversity: "Hell is the best place to practice because it makes you so much stronger."

Also, as mentioned above, all of us face the four challenges: illness, aging, death, and the loss of loved ones. If you practice Aikido, there is no guarantee, for example, that you will always be free from disease. You may well get very sick physically (and psychologically) for some reason and Aikido philosophy can help you with a "mind cure"—accepting the illness as challenge, seeking its source, working with it, and not being defeated (even though it may ultimately kill you). Over the years, I have trained with people who had severe physical problems (people who were missing limbs, were blind or deaf, or had Hodgkin's disease, etc.) and the primary obstacle was never their "disability" but their attitude. If they were determined to "obtain true victory" (*masakatsu*), they could use Aikido philosophy to adjust and adapt. Fear and worry can make you sicker than any physical disease. The secret to good health and longevity is, according to Aikido, "a pure heart and few desires."

Master Ueshiba left these encouraging words:

> Aikido is medicine for a sick world. We want to cure the world of the sickness of violence, malcontent, and discord—this is the Path of *aiki*. There is evil and disorder in the world because people have forgotten that all things emanate from one source. Return to that source and leave behind all self-centered thoughts, petty desires, and anger.

3

Aikido As Tantra

Tantra—the ancient science of realization and the art of living—is an eclectic system that exists in some form in nearly every culture, although it is most often identified with Indian, Chinese, and Tibetan thought. Aikido, too, is a very broad-based philosophy:

> Aikido has room for all of the world's eight million gods, and I cooperate with them all. The Great Spirit of *aiki* enjoins all that is divine and enlightened in every land.

Tantra teaches that the human being is a microcosm of the universe: "One who realizes the truth of the body realizes the truth of the universe. What is here is there; what is not here is nowhere." This insight lies at the heart of Aikido philosophy. Master Ueshiba, who was initiated into Shingon Buddhism (the Japanese form of Tantra) as a young man, boldly declared after his awakening, "I am the Universe!" He also said:

> Each one of us is a miniature universe, a living shrine.

> If you have life in you, you have access to the secrets of the ages, for the truth of the universe resides in each and every human being. All the principles of heaven and earth are living inside of you.

> The heart of a human being is no different from the soul of

heaven and earth. In your practice always keep your mind centered on the interaction of heaven and earth, water and fire, yin and yang.

One of the meanings of Tantra is "weave." In this sense, the word is quite close to the Aikido concept of *musubi*, "the process of linking things together." In Tantra, nothing is neglected or negated; everything is accepted but then transformed into something meaningful and whole. Similarly, in Aikido we learn to deal with every possible kind of attack (physical and mental) and to turn it into a positive experience. The Tantric path to realization is shorter and quicker than conventional ways, but more precipitous and perilous—the attempt to transmute base passions into golden enlightenment is said to be akin to walking on the sharp edge of a razor. Just as in Aikido—which employs martial art techniques that can be lethal if misused—lack of self-discipline and the slightest deviation from the proper framework can have grave consequences.

The Way of Aikido and the Path of Tantra both begin with action, in the form of physical and mental techniques. During training one must be devoted to the teaching and its teachers. Partial, limited, and secondary views must be abandoned, along with petty faultfinding, in order to concentrate on the essential message contained within the techniques.

In a narrower sense, Tantra means "skillful technique," and its primary focus is the unification or the synthesis of body, mind, and speech. In Aikido, the individual warm-up exercises, sequences performed with a sword and wooden staff, and techniques practiced with a partner are *asana*, yogic postures, utilized to develop the body. The body is all that we really possess and all we need to possess. As the Buddha taught:

In this very body, six feet in length, with its sense impressions and its thoughts and ideas, are the world, the origin of the world, the ceasing of the world, and the Way that leads to liberation.

Master Ueshiba said,

One does not need buildings, money, power, or status to practice Aikido. Heaven is right where you are standing, and that is the place to train. Establish yourself as a living Buddha image.

There is a powerful visualization technique used by Hasidic Jews to transform the body into the divine image:

Act well, and you will be like the right hand of God;
avoid evil, and you will be like the left hand of God;
do not look at ugliness, and you will have God's eyes;
do not listen to lies, and you will have God's ears;
do not smell rottenness, and you will have God's nose;
do not speak ill of others, and you will have God's mouth;
love creation, and you will have God's heart.

The formal stances assumed in training, called *mudra* in Tantra and *kamae* in Aikido, are meant to foster a proper state of mind. The basic Aikido stance—feet triangularly based, spine straight, fingers charged with *ki*, head centered, the eyes not focused on one particular thing, but rather taking in the entire field of vision—is strong, flexible, and receptive. With such an attitude, the teachings can be more easily assimilated.

In both Tantra and Aikido, the body needs to be a fit vessel. In order to perceive the world properly, the six sense organs (eyes, ears, nose, tongue, body, and mind) have to be cleansed. Master Ueshiba said:

If the senses are clogged, one's perception is stifled. The more it is stifled, the more contaminated the senses become. Free the six senses and let them function without obstruction, and your entire body will glow.

Master Ueshiba also recommended purification of the five viscera (heart, lungs, liver, spleen, and kidneys) and the six internal organs (stomach, large intestine, small intestine, gall bladder, urinary bladder, and *sansho* [a "floating" set of organs with no equivalent in Western medicine]).

In Aikido, such purification is accomplished through *misogi* and *kokyu-ho* breathing exercises. *Misogi* connotes cleansing, purification, and renewal. It is a combination of baptism—being "born again," "cleansed of sin," "initiation"—and anointing—being "consecrated," "blessed," or "infused with divine grace." Master Ueshiba said:

Misogi is a washing away of all defilements, a removal of all obstacles, a separation from disorder, an abstention from negative thoughts, a radiant state of unadorned purity.

Misogi of the body involves cleansing with water. Formal *misogi* takes place in the ocean, at the junction of two streams, or under a waterfall, but the simple act of washing away bodily dirt and grime with water is also *misogi*, as is sweating out impurities and toxins in a steam bath or during a vigorous workout. After the body is clean, warmed up, and relaxed, the mind can be prepared.

Misogi of the mind requires separation from malicious, negative, or petty thoughts. Then visualization techniques can be used to create the proper frame of mind. Tantric visualization can be quite complex, sometimes involving minute recreation of the cosmos, but in Aikido the technique is simple and clear. Here are Master Ueshiba's instructions:

> Sit comfortably and first contemplate the manifest realm of existence. This realm is concerned with externals, the physical form of things. Then fill your body with *ki* and sense the manner in which the universe functions—its shape, its color, and its vibrations. Breathe in and let yourself soar to the ends of the universe; breathe out and bring the cosmos back inside. Next, breathe up all the fecundity and vibrancy of the earth. Then, blend the breath of heaven and the breath of earth with that of your own, becoming the breath of life itself. As you calm down, naturally let yourself settle in the heart of things. Find your center, and fill yourself with light and heat. Keep your mind as bright and clear as the vast sky, as deep as the great sea, and as majestic as the highest peak.

In Aikido, visualization usually centers on the natural world. Of course, the exact theme of visualization depends on one's environment. Master Ueshiba lived in Japan, a mountainous island, but if he had been born in Arizona, for example, the ideal image would have been: "Keep your mind like the brilliant sunset, the endless expanse of desert, and the radiant red rocks."

This type of visualization is called *chinkon* (calm down) -*kishin* (returning to the source). In meditation one must first calm and settle down in order to return to the source, to merge with the Tao. (The Hebrew word *teshuvah* is usually translated as "repentance," but its actual meaning is "return to the source." Since we all are easily estranged from the divine essence, the Kabbalah teaches, we need meditation and visualization techniques to bring us back to the center.) Master Ueshiba taught that twenty minutes was a good length for the *chinkon* portion, and that *kishin* could last as long as forty minutes. However, *chinkon-kishin* should be a natural process of quiet assimilation, and should not be strictly timed.

Master Ueshiba mentioned another kind of meditation, which he called *odo no kamuwaza*. He said that *odo* connotes the idea of being "settled in emptiness." (*Kamuwaza* means "divine techniques.") This is akin to a Zen koan, for how can one be settled in something that does not exist? Perhaps *odo no kamuwaza* is a natural state of abiding in the source, free (empty) of conscious effort. In that state, wondrous techniques spontaneously emerge, whether one is standing, sitting, moving, or sleeping.

Ultimately, *misogi* of body and mind is meant to wash away distinctions—betwen outside and inside, body and mind, self and other, form and emptiness. *Misogi* is also meant to remove the physical and psychological obstacles that block the way, to increase pure awareness, and to make one whole.

Breathing techniques (*kokyu-ho*; known as *pranayama* in Yoga) are directed more toward cleansing of the internal organs. Deep inhalations fill the body with cleansing *ki* and forceful exhalations expel both physical and mental toxins. *Kiai* was mentioned in the previous chapter as a powerful explosion of energy, but it also can be used as a purification technique. In Aikido, there is a technique known as *happo-giri*, or "sword cuts in eight directions." Each cut—which can be executed with a live blade, a wooden sword, or a hand-sword—is accompanied by an explosive *kiai* that should emanate from deep inside you. Everything that is a source of anger, upset, or stress—everything that is holding you back—should be vehemently expelled with a loud shout. (The approach is not that far removed from a scene common in medieval Western painting: the devil being forced out from a tormented soul's mouth during an exorcism.)

Actually, we are always performing *kiai* simply by breathing: the inhalation (in Japanese, *su*; in Sanskrit, *sah*) and the exhalation (*haku*; *ham*) form *suhaku* (*soham*), the mantra that means "I am THAT!" Or, in Aikido terms, "I am the Universe!" Our individual breath is part of the universal breath. Breath is always with us, when we are awake or asleep, and it links us to— and sustains and renews—the cosmos.

In this context, Master Ueshiba often spoke of *aun no kokyu*. *Aun* is the Japanese equivalent of *om*, the ultimate sound of all Yogic and Tantric systems. *Om* is, in essence, the supreme mantra that covers the entire range of sound. Actually composed of the sounds A-U-M, *Om* reflects the cosmic order of creation, sustenance, and destruction; male, female, and neuter; past, present, and future; and waking state, sleep state; and dream state. In Aikido, *aun no kokyu* means to "breathe it all up"; in other words, to live completely and totally in the present. *Aun no kokyu* is the dynamic breath that energizes all the different forms of *kiai*.

Every *kiai* is a *kototama* ("word spirit"). Like Tantra, Aikido has a special science of sounds. The esoteric aspect of *kototama* employs a variety of esoteric chants and incantations. These have been presented in *The Essence of Aikido*, but the following is a further description linking the *kototama* of existence—A, O, U, E, I—to specific Tantric *chakra* in the body.

Chakra are "junctions of life energy" located in the human body. The number of *chakra* varies from four to twelve, in different systems. Aikido distinguishes four *chakra*, which are the head, throat, heart, and navel (lower body). These four are common to all schools of Tantra, and correspond to the brain, the lungs, the heart, and the stomach. The head *chakra* is the source of insight, the throat *chakra* is the source of soothing sounds, the heart *chakra* is the source of loving feelings, and the belly *chakra* is the source of vital energy. The head (*ajna* in Sanskrit) *chakra* is centered in the forehead, where the "third eye" of Asian iconography is placed. Before the first sound is uttered, its initial image springs forth from deep within one's consciousness. This "unstruck sound" evolves into the seed syllable A, symbolizing the beginning of all things, activated by the throat (*visuddha*) *chakra*. The next *kototama*, O, representing ceaseless flow, infinity, and perfection, emanates from the heart (*anahata*) *chakra*. The *kototama* U, the sound of birth and creation, resonates from deep inside the belly, from the solar plexus (*manipura*) *chakra*. The body then fills with the *kototama* E, which "branches out," vivifying our limbs. The *kototama* I, the breath of life, radiates from every pore, creating a vibrant energy field.

This kind of *kototama* exercise is designed to energize and heal the body, increase one's awareness of the power of sound, and harmonize one with the cosmic vibrations that sustain the world. Through this kind of practice, it is believed that *kototama* will eventually be manifest. That occurs when what you say, what you think, and what you are merge as one. (Since this is Tantra, much of it lies beyond words, and cannot be "explained." It can, however, be grasped intuitively through actual practice which is augmented by *kuden*, or "personal heart-to-heart instruction from a skilled teacher.")

While the esoteric aspects of *kototama* are intriguing, we must be equally concerned with the exoteric aspects of *kototama*: "kind words and gentle speech." Words are weapons. The Talmud states, "To shame someone in public is akin to murder." Gandhi wrote, "An evil word may be more dangerous than the actual violence of the moment." Indeed, most of us have been far more deeply wounded by something that was said to us than by a punch in the nose or a slap in the face. It is usually easier to get over a blow to the body than a cutting remark. If we really understand *kototama* we learn to choose our words carefully and with consideration.

Master Ueshiba was famous for his furious outbursts. But even his tirades could be thought of as "kind words and gentle speech," since anyone scolded by the Master never forgot it and would never make the mistake that prompted it again, and so would have learned a valuable lesson. However, when Master Ueshiba lectured on the philosophy of Aikido, his voice was calm and he was constantly smiling. At the beginning of training, Shirata-sensei would talk about Aikido philosophy for ten or fifteen minutes in a soothing, reassuring manner. Those little talks were as important as the incredibly powerful *kototama-kiai* shouts he taught us later. (Like most great masters, neither Morihei Ueshiba or Rinjiro Shirata wrote much themselves. It is up to the disciples to listen carefully, learn from what the master is saying, and then transmit the teaching faithfully. This kind of oral instruction, another aspect of *kototama*, is very important in every spiritual tradition. Buddhist sutras, for example, begin with the phrase, "Thus I have heard." Of course, each disciple hears things somewhat differently, based on his or her own level of experience and understanding, which explains why there is always so much diversity of interpretation in every spiritual tradition, even though the teaching all comes from the same source.)

At the last seminar he gave, Shirata-sensei watched one of the students perform a technique. At the end he said with a smile, "*Yoroshii*," which means "Well done!" but here also functions as a *kototama* that says, "How nice that you are practicing Aikido and doing your best!" The best *kototama* is joyous laughter—the most pleasing of sounds. I have a CD of traditional Hawaiian music that contains a short track of the musicians (Richard Hoopi'i and Ledward Kalapana) laughing. During the recording session, they made a funny mistake, and burst out laughing. The producer wisely included that segment at the end of the CD. Their harmonious and melodious laughter is truly sweet *kototama* a striking of the right chord that animates all who hear it.

Speaking of musical *kototama*, there is this instructive story. Following the Vatican reforms of the 1960s, a group of French Benedictine monks fell seriously ill not long after they were instructed to "modernize" their prayer routine and abandon their ancient Latin chants. They were given better food and more sleep but this still did not make them well. Finally the abbot allowed the monks to go back to their old schedule and let them conduct the daily office in Gregorian plainchant. They were all cured within nine months. (The beauty and healing property of chant is now recognized the world over.)

An important Tantric concept in Aikido is that of the red and white jewels. On the level of the human body, the jewels can be said to represent the red ova of the mother and the white sperm of the father. The conjunction of these jewels creates life, with the red jewel evolving into the internal organs, the flesh, and the skin, and the white jewel shaping the bone and marrow. In addition, blood must maintain a proper balance between red and white blood cells to remain healthy. On the level of the mind, the red and white represent the two great principles: feminine and masculine, yin and yang, water and fire. The union of male and female brings the world into being. In terms of Tantric alchemy, mercury (white jewel) is construed as Shiva's sperm, and sulfur (red jewel) is taken to be Parvati's orgasmic vaginal secretions. Mercury is too unstable and toxic to be used alone; for the process of alchemy to occur white male mercury must be bound to red female sulphur.

Aikido also shares the Tantric belief that in addition to the red and white jewels, a third jewel is needed for conception: a conscious soul. In Buddhism and Hinduism, the conscious soul exists and functions within the context of transmigration. In Aikido and the Kabbalah, the conscious soul is thought to be "called" or "summoned" from a higher realm. In either case, the "direct spirit" (Aikido) or the "divine spark" (Kabbalah) is present at conception. Thereafter, the body is gradually created, formed, and then "made into an image of God" at birth: a complete human being, with a destiny to fulfill.

Tantra is usually identified exclusively as the sexual practice of uniting male and female. This is unfortunate, since there is much more to Tantra than sex. Tantra involves the senses, and sex is a rich area for exploration of Tantric truth, but Tantric sex is not for the sensualist; Tantra requires discipline, forbearance, and trust. Sex is a valid philosophical pursuit. Pythagoras, who has been mentioned often, fell in love with Theano, one of his pupils. Their love affair created a scandal, but Theano went on to become a philosopher in her own right, thus vindicating her mentor/lover—he accomplished his goal of turning a student into an independent thinker. Sexual harmonization is important in Aikido as well—in Chinese sex manuals, the characters for *aiki* are used to refer to the ultimate sexual experience, of the male and female completely integrated in blissful intercourse.

Aiki sex seeks the elimination of male-female antagonism—a couple must learn to protect and shield each other—and the harmonization of all opposing principles: positive and negative, dynamic energy and receptive energy, individual soul and universal soul, space and time, fire and water, and samsara and nirvana. Once a couple comes truly together—progressing from excitement through engagement, consummation, and transcendence—there is a continuous exchange of *aiki*. From this delightful and holy union of male and female arises a pure knowledge, a knowledge that explains the nature of all things. In English, we speak of "carnal knowledge" disparagingly, but in fact human beings can really get to know each other (and themselves as well) when they make love—on the highest levels, it can even be a knowledge like never before.

Onisaburo Deguchi (1871–1947), Master Ueshiba's Omoto-kyo guru, wrote:

All religion is based on love, the love between a man and a woman.

Everyone, even the greatest of saints, comes into this world through an act of sex. Sex is our nature from birth to death. Thought itself originates in this union of two. The harmonious mingling of male and female gives birth to heaven and earth. The true form of heaven and earth is a couple in ecstatic union.

Sex makes it possible for human beings to enjoy an eternal spring. If you do not remain young at heart, you cannot enter paradise. Regarding sex, a human being should always imagine him- or herself as a vigorous thirty-year old in the prime of life.

Onisaburo stressed the fact that each sex has attributes of the other, and that it is not good to overemphasize the polarity of male and female. (Onisaburo himself said that he was a female spirit in a male body.) In the same vein, certain Taoist sects perform an initiation ritual of "mutual integration." The male and female partners dance slowly, alternating between the active and passive roles, reflecting the belief that both sexes share various qualities.

As in Tantra, Aikido philosophy considers every action to have three dimensions: the manifest, hidden, and divine (these are sometimes referred to as the external, internal, and essential). The manifest form of an Aikido technique is the physical execution: stance, grip, movement of the body. The hidden form of a technique is experienced in the anticipation of an attack through intuition, direction of the flow of *ki* energy, and mental, rather than physical, control. The third dimension is harder to describe. This is the dimension that links the technique to a "higher" realm. For example, in the performance of the *ikkyo* (number one) pin—perhaps the most fundamental Aikido technique—the body movements are simple and precise (manifest), but the attack must be countered at just the right instant, and the attacking force must be smoothly redirected without hesitation (hidden). The divine, or essential, dimension lies in the perfect control—both self-control and control of the situation—that is required. Perfect control is very hard to achieve, and that is the reason *ikkyo* is so difficult to do well—in other words, the simplest technique is also the hardest.

The three dimensions can also be expressed with the terms literal, allegorical, and mystical. These terms make clearer the connection to the arts—especially storytelling, literature, and poetry.

Human life also has three levels of meaning. The manifest form is our external existence: born here, lived there, died in that place. The hidden form would be our inner life of imagination, dreams, and mental pleasure (and pain). The divine form would be our ultimate purpose. Master Ueshiba has said:

> Everyone has a spirit that can be refined, a body that can be trained in some manner, a suitable path to follow. You are here for no other purpose than to realize your inner divinity and manifest your innate enlightenment.

As mentioned earlier, Master Ueshiba said that the merging of the red and white jewels created a third jewel, the jewel of pure consciousness. The unfolding of pure consciousness is the *raison d'etre* of all Aikido and Tantric practice. This consciousness springs forth from *ku*, emptiness:

> If you have not
> Linked yourself
> To true emptiness,
> You will never comprehend
> The full dimensions of Aikido.

Master Ueshiba called the physical manifest of true emptiness *sumikiri*, "perfect clarity of body and mind." Such an exalted state belongs to a different realm—the realm of the *siddhas* (accomplished masters) who possess seemingly miraculous powers. Master Ueshiba was such a *siddha* and he shared the grand Tantric vision of the Seventh Dalai Lama (1708–57):

> See the body as a temple of a deity.
> View the world as a sacred place.
> Hear all sounds as mystical music.
> Think like a buddha of bliss.

4

Aikido and Art

Onisaburo Deguchi taught Master Ueshiba that "art is the mother of religion" and that "God is the First Artist." (One of the meanings of the Greek word *kosmos* is "ornament.") Kukai (774–836), founder of Shingon Buddhism in Japan, wrote: "Eternal truth transcends color, but only by means of color can it be understood. Art is what reveals to us the state of perfection." The medieval German mystic Meister Eckhart (1260–1327) wrote: "Art is religion, religion art, not related but the same." In Islam it is said: "God is beautiful and loves beauty." The Hasidic master Reb Elimelekh (1717–86) taught: "When we see something beautiful, or eat something delicious, be aware that beauty and taste are God himself." Andre Malraux (1901–76) said: "Every masterpiece is a purification of the world."

Onisaburo was himself one of the most versatile artists of the twentieth century. He composed hymns, folk songs, love ballads, and even a few waltzes and tangos. He acted in plays and movies that he wrote and directed, and was an excellent costume designer. (He was likely the best, and certainly the most creatively dressed man in Japan during his day. Onisaburo did not weave cloth—this was about the only art he did not do—but his wife Sumiko and daughter Naohi did, creating the *Tsuruyama kusaki-zome* weave, colored with natural dyes made from pine needles, nettles, peach blossoms, chrysanthemums, eggplant, and tomato and set with mineral water from a valley near Mount Tsuru.) He did sculpture as well but he truly excelled at the traditional Japanese arts of poetry composition, calligraphy, ink painting, and pottery.

Incidentally, Onisaburo said that the most beautiful thing in creation was a woman's body, which he described like this:

> A wondrous thing, possessing mountains, hills, valleys, and a deep crevice surrounded by a field of soft grass.

The next most beautiful thing was the body of a man. Third was the body of a stallion.

Here is a typical poem by Onisaburo:

> When you listen quietly
> To the sound of
> A murmuring stream,
> You will hear
> God's whisper.

Onisaburo brushed thousands of pieces of calligraphy and hundreds of paintings for his followers and friends. His brushwork was spontaneous, dynamic, and free-flowing. Once he accidentally spilled ink over the paper he was going to use and, without missing a beat, then splashed water on the paper, pulled on the sides to spread the mixture around to create a hazy moon surrounded by dark clouds.

Regarding painting, Onisaburo had this to say:

> When I paint a landscape, I imagine myself sporting among the rocks and trees. When I paint a waterfall, I feel myself cascading down the paper. When I paint an animal, I always do the nose first so the creature can breathe. When I brush a human face, I like to paint in the eyes at sunrise so they will shine like the sun. I consider my paintings living entities.

Onisaburo said that you should lose yourself in your paintings and follow the divine impulse:

> Even the most
> Skillful artist

Does nothing more
Than copy
Divine creation.

Once at an exhibition of his art, Onisaburo overheard a viewer remark, "I can't believe the same person did all these different kinds of paintings!" Onisaburo said to him, "You are right. I was a different person each time I painted." This is very similar to Master Ueshiba's reply to a request to record his techniques on film: "Fine, but tomorrow they will be different."

Late in life, Onisaburo turned to pottery and produced several thousand *Yowan* ("Scintillating Teabowls"), decorated in bright, sometimes psychedelic, colors. (Critics joked that you needed sunglasses to look at them.) These tea bowls seem to have come from a different realm—many of them are simply named "Paradise No. 1" and so on down the line—and are not only beautiful but useful—tea can actually be drunk from them.

The goal of Omoto-kyo was to turn all daily actions into works of art. Everyone was encouraged to be a poet, a calligrapher, a dancer, a singer, a potter, a weaver, a farmer, a gardener, and a chef.

Onisaburo composed this poem:

Those who are not
Awakened to the
Joy of art will never
Make the dream of a heaven
On earth come true!

If someone had difficulty believing in the divine, Onisaburo said to him,

Look at a flower. How beautiful and colorful it is. How fragrant.
How many different kinds of flowers there are! Is this not divine,
the work of a great artist?

In addition to the art of Aikido, Master Ueshiba devoted himself to the arts of poetry composition, calligraphy, and farming.

In regard to calligraphy, interesting research has been conducted by Professor Tanchu Terayama, Headmaster of the Zen Brush Society (*Hitsuzendo*), on the relationship between *ki* and artistic beauty. He took dated works by the famous Zen calligrapher and master swordsman Tesshu Yamaoka (1836–88) and had portions of the writing magnified fifty thousand times with an electron microscope to study the "*ki* particles" in the ink. (When magnified so highly, the ink can be seen as individual particles.) The particles in Tesshu's very earliest pieces were dispersed and lackluster but in the ensuing years the particles clearly became rounder, richer, and more connected. In the last year of his life, the *ki* particles in Tesshu's brushwork were extraordinarily deep and vibrant. Terayama then magnified portions of calligraphy on "Tesshu" fakes (Tesshu's calligraphy is very valuable and imitations abound) and found, not surprisingly, that the ink particles in the fakes were very dull and weak. This is scientific "proof" of the insight that it is *ki* that animates a work of art.

Good brushwork is truly alive. I am fortunate to work in an environment surrounded by calligraphy brushed by Tesshu, the Buddhist nun Rengetsu (1791–1875), Jigoro Kano (1860–1938, founder of Judo), Onisaburo, Master Ueshiba, and other masters; their presence—their *ki*—is palpable and ever-inspiring. Good calligraphy nourishes the spirit, and is even thought to possess healing properties. (Picasso said that if we really understood art, we could create paintings that could cure toothaches.) Once I slept on a *tatami* mat next to an alcove in which hung a painting by the great Zen master Hakuin (1686–1768). All night I had powerful visions of direct instruction from that Master. The Japanese collector Masako Shirasu (1910–98) said that some of the pieces in her collection had given her "fifty years of dreams."

It is not difficult to see how *ki* is manifest in the calligraphy and painting of the Far East, but since *ki* is a universal force it should be present in all kinds of art, East or West. Indeed, one of the criteria of beauty everywhere is "to manifest vitality." For this to occur, there needs to be *aiki* between the artist and his or her creation. Tradition has it that prior to painting a landscape, the famous Zen artist Sesshu (1420–1506) would first contemplate the sea and mountains from his studio window. After drinking a cup of rice wine, he would play his bamboo flute until his mind was properly composed. Only then would he put brush and ink to paper. In the West, Dante (1265–1321) said: "One who paints a figure cannot draw it if one does not become it." Thomas Aquinas (1225?–74) defined beauty as "perfection, harmony, and clarity." In true art, a pleasant harmony exists between the artist, the art, and the viewer (or listener).

Let's consider the process of artistic creation. In classical Hindu aesthetics, an artist is often described as a being a yogi, one who joins a mental image with physical matter. Picasso (1881–1973) said, "I paint things as I think of them, not as I see them." William Blake (1757–1827) said, "As a man is, so he sees." The artist—a sculptor, for instance—first sits quietly and meditates on the image he wants to create. (In Aikido, this would be called *nen*, "fixing an ideal thought." In Tantra, the initial meditation is on the "original purity of the one spirit." A Buddhist artist summons up the four modes: friendliness, compassion, sympathy, and equinamity.) The stone he will work with has already been carefully selected, set on sacred grass, and anointed with milk. Offerings of flowers, fruit, and incense have been set before it. His chisels have been cleaned, sharpened, and consecrated. He gazes at the stone and then marks the central spot, the *bindu* point, from which the image will radiate. As he works, basically within the limits of classical forms but not slavishly bound to these forms, he is simultaneously aware of the tiniest details and the entire piece, and skilfully balances the parts with the whole. Indeed, the sculptor becomes the sculpture as the work progresses. The eyes are the last to be completed, and when they are painted in, a ritual of "giving the breath of life"—or the infusion of *ki*—is conducted to make the image real.

In terms of Aikido, the "stone" a practitioner works with is the Aikido partner, to be treated with dignity and respect. The tools are techniques, and prior to executing the techniques one must become centered. The classical forms of Aikido are performed within the context of that particular time and place, with appropriate adaptation; the distinction between attacker and defender is transcended. The entire process is the art of Aikido—an ideal fusing of spirit and technique.

If it is a true image, it will delight and inspire all those who gaze upon it, and become a valuable aid and support for those who are seeking knowledge. Good art always increases our awareness of some aspect of life, reveals something to us that we had not seen before, or liberates us from conditioned perception. An image allows us to take in universal truth in a concrete, accessible way. The absolute truth would be beyond comprehension —and representation—so it needs to be refracted. According to Tibetan tradition, the Buddha consented to have his image painted but when the artists attempted to do so they were too overwhelmed by his radiant and sublime presence to draw anything. The Buddha then suggested that they move the portrait session to a site next to a pond, so that they could paint his reflection.

Images also possess *ki*—we often speak of "flowing lines" in a sculpture or statue—and, indeed, recordings of certain Hindu and Buddhist images in Asia, ancient Egyptian statues, and megalithic stones in Europe have shown that these objects produce ultrasonic vibrations. The best examples of both pictorial and three-dimensional art appear to have been "crystalized"— emanating from *nen*, as we would say in Aikido—rather than created. In both East and West, there are images believed to be an "icon not made by human hands," perhaps for this reason. Other images are so realistic that people actually fall in love with them, going so far as attempting to have sex with them. (In Japanese folklore, there are a number of sex-with-a-statue tales with varying results; sometimes the offending party is punished with death and sent to hell; sometimes the statue comes to life and makes the devotee's dreams come true.)

We have many portraits of Master Ueshiba, painted by well-known artists of the day. Most are likenesses, but Master Ueshiba also asked an artist named Joyo Nozawa (1866–1937) to paint him in his ideal form as Ame no Mura Kumo Kuki Samuhara Ryuo. The artist had a very difficult time conjuring up a proper image of a Dragon King and struggled with it for several days, finally spending an entire night in meditation. Once the image came to him, however, he was able to complete the painting in less than an hour. Several busts were made of Master Ueshiba during his life. Once when he was shown a model of a bust before final casting, he astonished the artist by telling him, "This muscle on the back is not quite right"—Master Ueshiba knew his own body so well that he could describe places he could not actually see.

In live performances by stage actors, dancers, and musicians there needs to be good *aiki* between performer and audience for the program to be a success. A person with superior stage presence uses *kokyu*, good timing, both to bring out the best in his or her own performance and to establish rapport with the audience. Zeami, the father of Noh theater, told his students, "An actor must be at his best when the audience is at its worst."

Dance is a universal art form. People everywhere have always danced—to communicate with the gods and goddesses, to ensure fertility, to celebrate, and for pure pleasure. Prior to training, Master Ueshiba would usually perform *kagura*, a sacred Shinto dance, with a fan, a sword, or a staff. The origin of *kagura* is traced to the divine dance of Ame no Uzume no Mikoto before the cave in which the Sun Goddess Amaterasu Omikami was hiding. Amaterasu had shut herself up—and thus deprived the world of sunlight—to pout over the bad behavior of her brother Susano no Mikoto. The dance of Uzume was divine but quite playful and erotic; her movements caused all the other deities to burst out in laughter. When Amaterasu peeked out to see what the commotion was all about, she was grabbed by the powerhouse deity Ame no Tajikarao no Kami, who had been stationed by the cave door for exactly that purpose, and the goddess's light was brought back to the world. Although the main purpose of Uzume's dance was to lure Amaterasu out of her cave, she did achieve a state of ecstasy "as if possessed by a divine spirit." Similarly, Master Ueshiba's *kagura* was performed to link himself to the spirit world.

Master Ueshiba enjoyed teaching sword movements to teachers of classical dance, and one day a dance teacher asked him to teach her the movements made with a *naginata*, or halberd. Originally, the *naginata* was used by warrior monks but over the centuries it became the weapon of choice for samurai women, and Master Ueshiba had never practiced with it. That did not deter him, however. He ordered a disciple to obtain a popular novel in which the hero, a warrior monk named Benkei, is a master of *naginata*, and place the book on the Shinto altar. Master Ueshiba then asked not to be disturbed for the rest of the day, and shut himself up in the *dojo*. When the dance teacher returned for her lesson, Master Ueshiba showed her a series of beautiful moves. Later, after the woman had performed them on stage, an amazed (female) *naginata* master said to her, "What wonderful techniques! Where did you learn them?" Morihei's puzzled disciples asked him how he had been able to master the *naginata* so quickly. "Benkei himself visited me while I was in a trance and taught me his secrets," was the reply. (It helped too, of course, that the movements of Aikido are based on universal patterns that can be applied, with some adjustment, to virtually any body art.)

All over the world, dance is believed to be a gift of the gods. In a vision during a solar eclipse on 1 January 1889, the Paiute shaman Wovoka "went to heaven and saw God and all the people who had died long ago. God told me to come back and tell my people they must be good and love one another, and not fight, steal, or lie. He gave me this dance to give my people." That dance, performed in a great circle around a central fire, became known as the Ghost Dance.

The hula is synonymous with Hawaiian culture; in fact the hula *is* Hawaiian culture. It is inconceivable to think of Hawaii as separate from the chants, songs, and movements of hula. Hula is simultaneously a form of worship, an oral history of the islands, a fertility cult, a system of healing and well-being, and a school of music, poetry, dance, and mime. In short, hula is the Hawaiian manifestation of Aikido, a completely integrated system that promotes the unification of body and mind. We can find many similar examples of dance serving as the heart of culture in other parts of the globe.

Music is integrally related to dance. Music is the purest form of *kototama*. The universe is essentially musical. Willam of Auverge (1180–1249) wrote:

> The order and magnificence of the universe is like a most beautiful canticle and the wondrous variety of its creatures a symphony of joy and harmony.

In the context of music, rhythm would be fire, and sound would be water. According to the experiments of Hans Jenny, a modern Swiss scientist and musician, musical tones form beautiful and orderly shapes when transmitted through smoke, fluid, or very fine powder, exactly as predicted in *kototama* theory.

Music can be used as a technique of Aikido. One evening while he was out contemplating the heavens, Pythagoras came upon an agitated young man who had been jilted by his lover. A nearby aulos player was playing fast and furiously, working the young man into such a frenzy that he started to yell out threats about setting fire to the woman's house. Rather than accosting the inflamed youth and creating a disturbance, Pythagoras went over to the musician and asked him to slow down the tempo and change to a quieter, more soothing tune. The musician did so, the young man calmed down, returned to his senses, and eventually went home without doing harm to the woman or himself.

Master Ueshiba himself did not play any musical instruments but he was a master chanter. Sometimes he would chant Omoto-kyo and Shingon prayers for an hour or more. Master Ueshiba's voice was rather high-pitched but very powerful. When he chanted with other Omoto-kyo followers in a group, Master Ueshiba's projection of the sounds was so strong that people sitting in front of him had to move because they felt as if someone was striking them repeatedly on the back.

The other art to which Master Ueshiba applied himself was farming. *Musubi*, or exuberant growth, is central to Aikido, and Master Ueshiba loved to raise all kinds of crops and flowers. The land at Iwama was rather poor, but the yield was always high because Master Ueshiba understood how to make the earth fertile and nurture the crops, without resorting to artificial and dangerous chemicals.

Traditional Pueblo Indian farmers still steadfastly reject the advice of American government agricultural agents to use steel plows to prepare their fields. The Indian farmers use digging sticks to plant in spirals starting from the center of the field. They maintained that the ground in springtime is just like a pregnant woman, in need of gentle treatment. Use of a cold steel plow would violate Mother Nature.

The preparation of food is also a fine art. *Oishii*, the Japanese word for delicious, literally means "beautiful taste." Master Ueshiba basically followed the Omoto-kyo diet of eating fish for increased wisdom, vegetables for compassion, and rice for bravery.

We mentioned that sexual union was one of the central themes of Tantra. Lovemaking is both a fine and a "martial" art—Cupid and Kama (the Hindu god of love) are both archers, expert at shooting arrows into the most difficult targets. Lovemaking is Aikido: "In union with a beloved partner, one becomes whole and complete." Aikido lovemaking involves mutual respect, serenity of heart, gentle yet powerful technique, and full engagement of the body and spirit.

A Tibetan medical manual describes the ideal environment for lovemaking like this:

The setting should be tranquil with a pond, stream, or waterfall. Flowers and greenery should abound, and the air filled with bird sounds. Both the man and woman should be clean, nicely dressed, soft spoken, and well-mannered. The food should include honey, milk, cream, sweets, meat broth. The lovemaking should include pleasant conversation, kissing, touching, embracing, and relaxation.

Here is more detailed advice from the Taoist sex manual *Joining Yin and Yang*:

Hold hands, and then begin stroking from the wrists. Proceed up the arms to the armpits, then around to the shoulders and neck. Lightly caress the neck, the hollow of the collarbone, the nipples, the belly, and the side of the body. Reaching the realm of the jade gate and the jade stalk, linger there for a while, and feel the energy. Hug and kiss, loosen up and have fun. After that, engage each other in one of the ten styles of sexual congress (tiger roaring, cicada clinging, inchworm, deer nudging with his antlers, phoenix rising, monkey climbing, toad, rabbit running, dragonfly, or fish feeding). During lovemaking, the vital spirit enters the internal organs and produces a wondrous glow.

In Aikido, we want all our techniques—and by extension, all our acts—to be "true, good, and beautiful" (in Japanese, *shin, zen, bi*; in Sanskrit, *satyam, shivam, sundram*). When we execute a technique it must be true, that is, precise, clean, and effective. It is good because the techniques are designed so that no one gets injured. Aikido must also be beautiful, pleasing both to perform and watch. (It is disheartening to witness how much ugliness has crept into modern *budo*—god-awful gaudy uniforms, horrible grimaces, and sloppy punching, kicking, pushing, and pulling.) When we think about art, whether fine, folk, or martial, the most pleasing examples are similarly true (well executed), good (meaningful), and beautiful (pleasing to the eye and the ear).

Master Ueshiba's perception of the world's beauty is well expressed by this lovely Navajo benediction:

In the Beauty before me, I walk.
In the Beauty behind me, I walk.

In the Beauty below me, I walk.
In the Beauty above me, I walk.
In the Beauty around me, I walk.
In the Beauty within me, I walk.
All is complete in Beauty.

5

Aikido and Global Society

One of the meanings of Aikido is "mutual accord." Aikido is never practiced for mere self-defense or individual spiritual development. Aikido is a social activity. There is no separation in Aikido training between people of different sexes, different colors, different sizes, and different ages. Everyone trains together, and you learn how to deal with all manner of human beings—big and small, young and old, hard and soft, flexible and stiff, athletic and clumsy, bold and tentative. There are no matches pitting one human being against another, and no contests consisting of flashy routines artificially constructed to garner a high score from a panel of judges. Everyone in the *dojo* takes turns being a "winner" and a "loser." Training in a *dojo* is meant to prepare us for the real challenge of practicing Aikido in daily life with our family, friends (and enemies), coworkers, and all the people with whom we come into contact.

Although the primary image of Master Ueshiba is that of an otherworldly mystic, far removed from the concerns of society, for the first fifty years of his life he was an ardent, even radical, social reformer. As a youth in Tanabe, he learned about the Buddhist activism of Kukai. In portraits, Kukai is depicted as a master of Tantric meditation, but he is as famed for his contributions to society as for his understanding of cosmic mysteries. Kukai established the first school in Japan for the nonaristocratic classes, he had bath houses built over the many curative hot springs he discovered around the country, and he served as chief engineer of a massive reservoir project.

Later, as a teenager, Morihei came under the influence of Kumagusu Minakata (1867–1941), one of the most progressive social thinkers in Japanese history.

Prior to settling in Tanabe, Minakata had lived overseas for sixteen years. The last eight of those years were spent in London, where he established himself as a scholar of unusual depth and breadth: he had at his command English, French, Italian, Spanish, Portuguese, Greek, Latin, Chinese, Arabic, Persian, and Japanese, of course, and he published research papers on a wide variety of subjects including botany, astronomy, anthropology, archaeology, and Oriental religions. In Tanabe, Minakata established a kind of peoples' university and, among many other things, lectured the local residents on the evils of industrial pollution, unbridled capitalism, and central government.

Minakata did not believe the development of coal and copper mines in Japan to be a good thing; pollution from the mines, he thought, would ruin streams and poison the land. Industrialization of the textile industry would make workers into wage slaves, and break them in body and spirit. A government plan to confiscate and develop property belonging to local shrines would result in the destruction of wildlife sanctuaries and essential watersheds, and would seriously disrupt traditional village life. Minakata was no ivory-tower intellectual—he was not afraid to go to jail for his beliefs, and in fact landed there after one particularly forceful protest. Minakata refused to be bailed out. "Why should people with money or rich friends be freed while the poor have to languish in jail? Everyone should be treated the same."

Even before coming under the influence of Minakata, Morihei had been protesting injustice. His first job was as an auditor at the local tax office but he quit this position in order to work on behalf of individual fishermen against the Fishery Industries Regulation Act. Certain wealthy operators and corrupt officials were unfairly using the new law to stifle competition. Morihei used his knowledge of the tax codes to defend the fishermen, at the same time protecting them against threats of violent reprisal. Later, Morihei teamed up with Minakata to oppose the national government's Shrine Consolidation Policy, through demonstrations and protests. From his experiences with Minakata, Morihei realized the value of wide-ranging knowledge and how important it was not to sit idle on the sidelines when his community was under threat.

The population of Tanabe was growing, and there was not enough farm and fishery work to go around. Morihei decided to take a group of fifty-two families, including his own, to the frontier land of Hokkaido. Morihei became a pioneer: building a village, organizing health, sanitation, and educational facilities, and establishing logging, horse-breeding, and pig-farming industries. He even ran for political office and won a seat on the village council.

After he left Hokkaido, Morihei joined the Omoto-kyo, which was as much a radical social movement as a religion. In fact, the whole purpose of Omoto-kyo was literally to create a "heaven on earth." Omoto-kyo was founded by Nao Deguchi (1836–1918), a desperately poor and troubled village woman. After she was visited by the god Konjin, Nao began preaching publicly in the name of that previously obscure deity. Nao's basic theme: "The time is come and the world needs to be completely cleansed and reformed! Emperors, kings, and all forms of artificial government must be done away with, and true equality established; abolish capitalism, return to the land, and do not let the selfish and greedy prosper at the expense of the righteous and diligent."

Later Nao teamed up with a young shaman named Kisaburo Ueda. Ueda married Nao's daughter Sumi and was adopted into the clan, taking the name Onisaburo Deguchi. Onisaburo's views were not as extreme as Nao's (Nao denounced schools, formal education, and *kanji* characters as great evils and refused to have her grandchildren vaccinated against smallpox since the vaccine came from an animal and had been developed in a foreign country) and his more flexible approach helped the Omoto-kyo movement gain great popularity. However, Onisaburo was no less adamant that society must be reformed:

> Armament and war are the means by which landlords and capitalists make their profit, while the poor must suffer. There is nothing in the world more harmful than war and more foolish than armament. The real fight is not against foreign adversaries but against those here at home who suppress our freedom, trample on our human rights, crush peace, and destroy our culture for the sake of profit.

Onisaburo spent a total of six-and-a-half years in prison for espousing such views, and his wife Sumi and many other Omoto-kyo leaders were also imprisoned for various lengths of time.

One day at the Omoto-kyo compound, a construction crew of ten men tried to reposition a large tree, but were unable to do so because of their dissension regarding the best procedure. Morihei came upon the scene and was struck by thoughts like, "Why can't people in Japan cooperate better?" and "Why do countries have to wage war against each other?" Agitated, Morihei grabbed the tree and singlehandedly moved it to its new location. Onisaburo was also present and said to Morihei, "That is the power of righteous indignation. Channel that tremendous force into the proper activity and you can accomplish much."

During the raid on Omoto-kyo in December 1935, an arrest warrant was issued for Master Ueshiba as well. Many of his disciples were high-ranking officials in the government and they were able to shield from him from imprisonment (but it seems that he was under house arrest for a time). They advised him to denounce Onisaburo to save his own skin, but Master Ueshiba refused to do so.

In light of his teachings on harmony and peace, many people wonder why Master Ueshiba did not oppose the war more strongly during the years 1935–45. His position was very difficult, particularly with a family to protect, but his message was consistent. Rinjiro Shirata, who was a live-in disciple before the war, clearly remembered Master Ueshiba telling his disciples that "killing is always a sin," unavoidable sometimes but never justified, and that *bushido* is "learning how to live, not learning how to die." That was the exact opposite of what the military government was drumming into the populace. Other prewar disciples have said: "If all those government officials had really understood what Master Ueshiba was teaching them, Japan would never have gotten into such a stupid war." Master Ueshiba once complained to his son Kisshomaru:

The military is dominated by reckless fools, ignorant of statesmanship and religious ideas, slaughter innocent citizens indiscriminately, and destroy everything in their path. They act in total contradiction to the will of the gods and they will surely come to a sorry end. True *budo* is to nourish life and foster peace, love, and respect, not to blast the world to pieces with weapons.

During the war, Master Ueshiba was always considered "soft" by the military police, and kept under surveillance. Behind the scenes, Master Ueshiba was involved in various peace initiatives but finally the only way he could protest was through noncooperation. In 1942, pleading illness, he resigned from all his public duties and secluded himself in Iwama. This stance is in sharp contrast to many other martial art instructors and religious leaders who vociferously insisted right to the end that Japan should fight to the last man, woman, and child, and not surrender.

Onisaburo, who had been released on bail in 1942, seemed to go into seclusion as well, but in fact continued his anti-war activities clandestinely. Onisaburo told Omoto-kyo followers who were drafted into the army that "the Gods do not love murderers" and "the Gods are never happy to see the sacrifice of a single human life." He instructed them to shoot their weapons into the air and to desert if they had an opportunity. To protect them from harm, he gave them talismans that read, with a touch of black humor, "Great Victory to the Enemy." Onisaburo sent secret messages to his followers in Japan, informing them of Japan's certain defeat and pointing out which parts of the country would be relatively safe. In 1942, during the darkest days of his country's history, the irrepressibly upbeat Onisaburo founded an "Optimist Society," Rakutensha. This was the same year that Master Ueshiba decided to call his art "Aikido."

Immediately after the end of the war Onisaburo composed this poem:

> Morning and evening
> Purify body and soul
> And pray to Heaven and Earth
> This is how to win
> Victory for our Nation.

After the war, Master Ueshiba stated that he knew that Japan was going to lose and that terrible weapons of destruction would fall on Hiroshima and Nagasaki. The atomic bombing of those two cities was a wake-up call for humankind, Master Ueshiba believed, and he wanted to prepare himself for the new era that would follow the end of war. Later, he expressed deep regret at having taught lethal techniques at the various military academies, and stated in an interview:

In the old days, martial arts were used for destructive purposes —to attack others in order to seize more land and possessions. Japan lost the war because it followed an evil, destructive path. From now on, martial arts must be used for constructive purposes.

Following a very active life in society, in the postwar years Master Ueshiba turned all the administrative duties of the Aikido organization to Kisshomaru and other senior disciples, and devoted himself to elaborating the philosophy of Aikido. Above all, he said, Aikido must become an agency of world peace:

> War must cease. We are all members of one big family; now is the time to eliminate fighting and contention. This world was created to be a thing of beauty. If there is no love between us, that will be the end of our home, the end of our country, and then the end of our world.

Peace is not just an absence of strife, but a state of wholeness and prosperity. Master Ueshiba gave this advice to world leaders:

> The real art of peace is not to sacrifice a single one of your warriors to defeat an enemy. Vanquish your foes by always keeping yourself in a safe and unassailable position; then no one will suffer any losses. The way of a warrior, the art of politics, is to stop trouble before it starts. It consists in defeating your adversaries spiritually by making them realize the folly of their actions.

There have been, alas, many dreadful conflicts since 1945, but also some hopeful signs. The Cold War has thawed and the threat of nuclear war has lessened. There are smaller, but significant, signs as well: a memorial in Okinawa honoring all the people, on both sides, who were slaughtered there during the fighting in World War II; and a U.S. military officer with Aikido training who served during the Gulf War telling his Aikido instructor proudly, "My unit captured our objective without loss of life on either side." Even if there were no such signs that the world was becoming more peaceful, we would still be optimistic—optimism is the essence of Aikido philosophy. Master Ueshiba's teacher Onisaburo lost everything twice through government suppression of the Omoto-kyo organization, his quixotic quest (undertaken with Morihei) to find Shambhala failed, and he was unjustly cast into prison for years, but hope and good humor never failed him. He made optimism one of the pillars of his faith:

> The purpose of religion is to make you feel joy in the depths of your being. Any religion that intimidates and menaces its followers is no religion at all. Pessimism, gloom, thoughts of sin, and abasement have no place in Omoto-kyo.

Master Ueshiba felt the same way about Aikido. Following Japan's crushing defeat, he was one of the few Japanese who were optimistic about the future. "Don't worry," he consoled his disheartened disciples:

> Instead of foolishly waging war, hereafter we will wage peace, the true purpose of Aikido. We will train to prevent war, to abolish nuclear weapons, to protect the environment, and to serve society.

Master Ueshiba believed that the principles of Aikido applied to the economy as well:

> The economy is the basis of society. When the economy is stable, society develops. The ideal economy combines the spiritual and material, and the best commodities to trade in are sincerity and love.

Master Ueshiba believed that democracy should be based on the Aikido concept of *masakatsu*: "The weakest have the same opportunity as the strongest." In a true democracy, ideas are integrated rather than fought over. Collaboration and harmonization are favored over competition and rivalry.

Harmony with nature is a central tenet of Aikido, and Master Ueshiba was particularly concerned with destruction of the environment. He was a longtime organic farmer, and on his visit to Hawaii in 1961 he pleaded with his students there—many of whom worked in agriculture—to do away with harmful chemicals for the crops.

On a more individual level, Master Ueshiba hoped that Aikido practitioners would strive to create a little heaven on earth each time they train in the *dojo*. The principles of Aikido—purity, serenity, gratitude, respect, harmony, love—are to be put into practice in each session. The techniques are ideal forms, to be employed as vehicles of realization; Aikido training should always result in *misogi*, a purification of body and mind.

In good Aikido training, we generate light (wisdom) and heat (compassion). Those two elements activate heaven and earth, the sun and moon; they are the subtle manifestations of water and fire. Unify the material and spiritual realms, and that will enable you to become truly brave, wise, loving, and empathetic.

Train hard, experience the light and warmth of Aikido, and be a real person. Train more, and learn the principles of nature. Aikido is becoming established all over, but it will have a different expression in each place it takes root. Continually adapt the teachings and create a beautiful pure land.

There is a Lakota Sioux Indian prophecy that one day all people, friend and foe alike, will sit down together in peace, united in a single great circle. Master Ueshiba also longed for such a day. Late in life he expressed this desire in various forms:

Come join hands with this old grandpa to unite the world. We have no enemies in Aikido, none of us are strangers. Every day, let's train to make the world a little more peaceful.

The divine beauty
of heaven and earth!
All creation,
Members of
One family.

The purpose of Aikido is unification: between body and spirit, male and female, self and others, man and nature, and the individual and society. The work of Aikido is to link things together, to make things resonate, to create a heaven on earth.

PART II

PRACTICE

Morihei Ueshiba, his body bristling with *ki*, demonstrates an amazing Aikido technique.

"Aikido begins and ends with respect." Rinjiro Shirata performs the formal Aikido bow made at the start and finish of every practice. This deep bow reflects the profound respect we have for the Aikido tradition, our training partners, and the *aiki* sword and *aiki* staff, as well as the gratitude we feel toward life itself, our ancestors, our fellow human beings, and the animals and plants that sacrifice themselves for our food. A scroll or signboard bearing the three characters *ai-ki-do* is always displayed in the *dojo*, as a constant reminder to practitioners to follow the Way of Harmony.

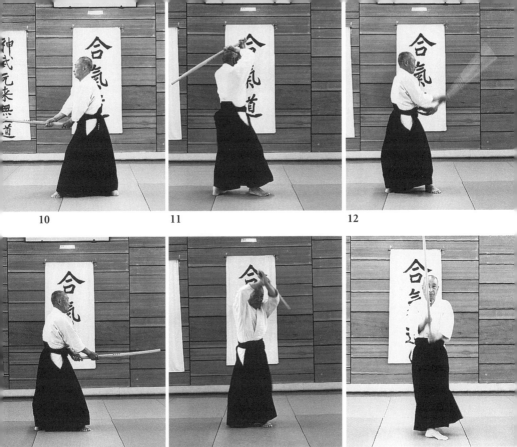

10   11   12

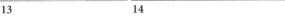

13   14   15

16

While this book is not a technical manual, we will look at the essential techniques of Aikido in terms of their philosophical significance. Here, Shirata-sensei performs *shiho-giri*, "four-directions cut." In addition to being a way to express gratitude in the four directions—each cut is actually a salutation—the cuts also represent the severing of all psychological bonds and the opening of a proper path for us to follow.

1

There are a variety of solo exercises such as *shiho-giri*, but to truly practice Aikido you need to work with a partner to assess your ability to harmonize yourself with a flesh-and-blood human being. This is the basic Aikido paired stance: a wrist grab that links, symbolically, the fire element (the left arm of the "attacker") with the water element (the right arm of the "defender"). A circuit is thus formed between the partners, with the grip as the central point of contact. Techniques can be executed in four "dimensions"—diamond, willow, flowing, and *ki*—and this series shows the diamond dimension, which is solid, stable, and precise. To illustrate the "gratitude" aspect of *shiho-nage* (four-directions throw), the author places his hands in the *gassho* mudra—a universal gesture of prayer and thanksgiving—and executes the technique. In regular training, partners take turns acting as attacker and defender, so that each person can experience both sides of the Aikido equation.

2

3

4

5

79

1

This sequence, taken from the Noma Dojo photo series shot in 1936, shows Master Ueshiba performing *irimi-nage* in the diamond dimension. He first avoids the attack by entering deeply to the side of his partner; he then immediately immobilizes the attacking arm while delivering an *atemi* (disarming blow) that stops short of actual contact. Such *atemi* is meant to cut through the attacker's spirit rather than his body. Next the master guides the attacker's head up and back, and steps in to complete the throw, all the while remaining in very close proximity to the partner. The final posture, known as *zanshin*, in this case resembles the stance assumed by Jesus Christ in many paintings depicting the raising of Lazarus from the dead. It is a healing posture rather than one indicating any threat of an additional strike. As illustrated here, sometimes the best way to deal with aggression is not to retreat, but to go right into its heart and disarm it at its core.

2

3

4

Smiling broadly, the eighty-four-year-old master demonstrates *irimi-nage*. Taking delight in training and having an optimistic outlook on life are two essential principles of Aikido philosophy.

Here we are back at the Noma Dojo. Master Ueshiba has "opened"—shifted his body to his partner's outside—to deflect the attack and put himself out of harm's way. His *atemi* is perfectly placed, and a slight cut downward with his left hand will knock his partner off balance and bring him all the way down to the mat. "To have an opening" where one is vulnerable to attack is not good, of course, but in Aikido, the concept of being "open" has the opposite meaning: one is open-minded and ready to deal with any kind of challenge that arises or to seize any opportunity that presents itself.

1

The previous technique consisted of only the *kai* (open to the side) movement. Here, Shirata-sensei combines *kai* opening with the *ten* turn. After stepping in, he makes a 180-degree turn, releases his hand from the partner's grip and applies *atemi* to draw out the partner's other arm so that he can hold both arms. Shirata-sensei turns his hips, then steps in and throws his partner. These kinds of *kaiten* movements form the heart of Aikido techniques. In the last public seminar that Shirata-sensei conducted, when he was eighty years old, his *kaiten* turns were spectacularly big and bold. He reminded me of a whirling dervish who does the "turn," dancing round and round as he visualizes an ascent to heaven. Philosophically as well, we always hope to turn things around our way.

2

3

4

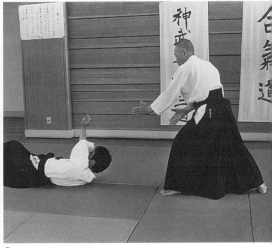

5

1

Kokyu, derived from concentrated breath control, is the power source of Aikido techniques. Here Shirata-sensei, at age seventy, lets a twenty-year-old college student grip his arm with full force. Shirata-sensei fills his entire body with *kokyu* and then slides forward, lifting the partner and completely dissipating the partner's strength. As shown here, breath power does not diminish with age the way that pure physical strength does. Breath power is the key to healthy living.

2

In Aikido we prefer not to use unnatural dead weights to build strength. Instead we ask our partners to graciously serve as living dumbbells so we can make the *kokyu* techniques more challenging by being held by two or more people. In some styles of Aikido, this kind of natural power is described more in terms of *ki* than *kokyu*. The two concepts are very closely related, but in essence *ki* is fundamental innate energy, while *kokyu* is concentrated and applied energy.

Kisshomaru Ueshiba demonstrates a *kokyu-nage* technique with his son, the current Doshu, or Headmaster, Moriteru Ueshiba. A second meaning of *kokyu* is "perfect timing." While the *kokyu* power techniques are of necessity static and precisely executed, *kokyu* throws are dynamic and free-flowing. One learns to adjust to all the subtle changes in a partner's moves and to apply techniques at just the right time. In human affairs, a similar sense of good timing is one of the most valuable assets a person can possess.

1

Shirata-sensei demonstrates a seated *ikkyo* pin, moving like a wave that crests up and then flows smoothly down. All the pins are variations on this one basic movement, and each variation is meant to stretch and stimulate different joints and muscles, thus promoting overall good health. Philosophically, the term *osae* is quite similar to the English expression "pin down"—to locate the exact source of a problem, or to force someone to make up his or her mind. It also symbolizes control—both control of a situation and control of the self.

2

3

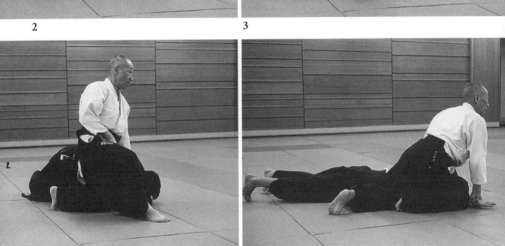

4

5

6

1

In Aikido, we always presume that attacks can come from any direction. Just as in real life, getting stabbed in the back is the hardest kind of attack to anticipate, so practice of *ushiro* techniques are an important part of the Aikido curriculum. Normally you would not allow anyone to get behind you this way, but for the sake of training Shirata-sensei lets a partner grasp his collar from the back. Shirata-sensei whirls to avoid simultaneous attacks from the back and front, throws one partner to the side, and stands ready to meet the challenge from the front. *Ushiro* techniques like these are meant to foster a "sixth sense" that can be very useful in everyday life.

2

3

1

In this *tenchi-nage* technique from the Noma Dojo series, the heaven and earth extension can be seen in each segment. In the first photograph, Master Ueshiba guides the attacking hand up toward heaven and uses *atemi* to drive his partners's body up as well. Master Ueshiba himself, however, is rooted to earth. In the second photograph, Master Ueshiba has lifted his partner up in a regular heaven and earth extension while the partner is in a reverse heaven and earth predicament—his head is pointing toward earth, and his feet toward heaven. In the third photograph, which shows the completed throw, Master Ueshiba assumes the heaven and earth *zanshin* posture.

2

3

While there is a special set of *tenchi-nage* techniques, the "heaven and earth extension" posture can be seen in many other techniques as well. Here Master Ueshiba executes *irimi-nage* with a heaven and earth movement.

In addition to being found in many kinds of martial art and dance forms, the *tenchi* posture is often seen in religious icons. This is a *tenchi* Jesus from a Catholic church in Holland. In this case, the *tenchi* posture can be interpreted as: "I carried God's teaching from heaven down to earth"; "My kingdom extends from heaven to earth"; or "Heaven and earth are linked through my body and blood." Notice also Jesus's sacred heart *chakra*.

In Aikido, we use the *bokken* (wooden sword) and *jo* (wooden staff) as "instruments of enlightenment." Most Aikido body movements parallel the clean and sharp movements of the sword, and the basic *kamae* is the *seigan* stance shown here. One meaning of *seigan* is "pure vision." (Others are "true vision," "clear vision," and "star vision.") The secret of Buddhist enlightenment is said to be the ability to "see things as they really are," free of preconceived notions and mental projections. In Aikido, too, we train to see things purely and truly. Master Ueshiba also said, "The stance of love is *seigan no kamae*," and for a time, he even took "Seigan" as his first name.

Here is a close-up of Shirata-sensei swinging the sword of *aiki* as he emits a magnificent *kiai*. Shirata-sensei called this kind of *kiai* the "breath of life shout." It should be of the same intensity as the cry that a baby makes at birth. As in Tantra, in Aikido practice we aim to harmonize the mind, body, and voice. In this photo it is clear that Shirata-sensei has achieved that ideal state.

(Left) While the movements of the *aiki* sword are sharp and decisive, the movements of the *aiki jo* are more free-flowing The sword symbolizes resolution; the *jo* symbolizes intuition. Prior to training, Master Ueshiba usually performed *misogi no jo* as a contemplative purification ritual. During the last five years of his life, Shirata-sensei developed his own *misogi no jo* that we continue to practice in Classical Aikido. This posture is the initial movement of that *misogi no jo*, called "sending forth of the spirit." (Above) The staff—as protective weapon or symbol of authority—is found in many different cultures. Here a petroglyph shows a Hawaiian warrior striking a classical *jo* posture.

One's outer form reflects the inner state. In these three photographs, we can see the manifestation of Master Ueshiba's different *mitama*, "souls." (Left) This image carries both Master Ueshiba's physical body and his transfigured form as Ame no Mura Kumo Kuki Samuhara Ryuo, the Dragon King peering over his shoulder. The presence of a *kushi-mitama*—a soul that is mysterious, profound, wise, and high-minded—is quite evident. (Above left) Master Ueshiba could be awe-inspiring at times, as here. His fierce, uncompromising *ara-mitama* has come forth, and he is on guard against sloppy or inattentive behavior. (Above right) In this calm and pleasing portrait we can sense both the peacefulness of the *nigi-mitama* and the brightness of the *sachi-mitama*.

As mentioned in Part I, Chapter 3, quiet contemplation, or *chinkon-kishin*, is central to Aikido. Life can be very distracting and confusing so it is helpful to have periods when you can "calm down and return to the source." Since we employ visualization, the eyes are closed, and the images are taken from nature—"Keep your mind like the vast sky, the highest peak, and the deepest ocean."

Meditation clears the mind and chanting purifies the voice. Master Ueshiba chanted various Shinto and Buddhist prayers every day, both inside and outdoors. Chanting is a natural human activity, universally practiced until the chaos of the twentieth century made it difficult (if not illegal) to engage in daily prayers in many places.

One meaning of *aiki* is "yoke," and Aikido can be considered a type of yoga. Yoga has *pranayama* exercises to develop breath power. In Aikido, we use *kokyu-ho* exercises to foster breath (and *ki*) energy. Here the author performs the breath of heaven movement, spreading his fingers like a plum flower in full bloom to receive the energy of the sky.

Book learning is also essential for the creation of a well-rounded philosophy. Morihei loved to study the Japanese religious classics. One of the things that most impressed me about Shirata-sensei was his lifelong devotion to learning. Even in his final years, he would often sit for hours reading a book, taking careful notes. He continually amazed me with his erudition on a number of diverse subjects which he liked to link to one Aikido principle or another.

Pythagoras was mentioned several times in Part I. He is the father of Western philosophy, a system that is sometimes believed to have little in common with the philosophy of the East. In fact, as was noted, there are many points of convergence between the "Western" thought of Pythagoras and the "Eastern" philosophy of Aikido. Human beings are essentially the same, and many differences are superficial and secondary. "Look for what is the same, not what is different" is one key to Aikido philosophy.

In this Russian Orthodox icon of the Madonna and Child, the stars intersect to form eight points, which we could interpret as the eight powers of Aikido. More interesting, however, are the stances of the angels surrounding Mary and the infant Jesus. They maintain postures very similar to *kamae* used in Aikido techniques. It is very unusual for me not to find an Aikido correspondence like this in any part of the world where I find myself, no matter how remote geographically or culturally.

Here is another example of perfect correspondence between the "mystical" philosophy of the East and the "scientific" philosophy of the West. Master Ueshiba often said: "The only way that I can truly explain Aikido is by means of the triangle, circle, and square." The inscription accompanying this alchemical diagram, printed in 1618, states: "From a man and woman create a circle, a square, a triangle, and then another circle and you will obtain the Philosopher's Stone [capable of turning base metal into gold]."

Every true philosophy must deal with the issue of sex—the source of life. As mentioned in Part I, *aiki* was the term used for the ultimate sexual experience in Chinese love manuals. In this sense, *aiki* represents the total integration, physically and spiritually, of two human beings. In Japan, *aiki* integration is achieved by the god Izanagi and the goddess Izanami, shown here communing on Mount Tsukuba. From their *aiki* union the nation of Japan came into being. The Shinto philosopher Masuho Zanko (1655–1742) declared, "The Way of the Gods is none other than the way of the union between man and woman."

In the human realm, the *aiki* union of two souls generates *musubi*, the creative life-force. This photograph is from a Belgian wedding. It is a tradition there for the bride and groom to entwine their fingers to symbolize their firm union. (*Musubi* also means tying together or knotting.) This is an example of *ki-musubi*, "the tying together of two forces," as well.

The author discusses the concept of *musubi* during an Aikido class in a *dojo* on the island of Hawaii, not far from the Kilauea Crater, abode of Madame Pele, the goddess of the volcano. Aikido teaches us to harmonize ourselves with our surroundings, and it is important to learn about, and be sensitive to, the local traditions of each place. (I always make a silent offering to Madame Pele and request permission to train in her domain.) And, naturally, the techniques take on a different cast in each place by incorporating the best elements of the local culture.

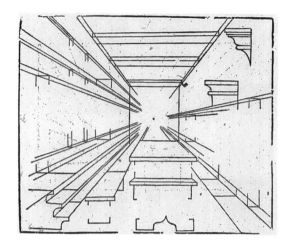

Master Ueshiba constantly reminded his students not to forget that all things emanate from One Spirit. This medieval diagram can be read both ways: all things emanating from one point and all things returning to one point. Artistic creation similarly unfolds from, and yet remains centered on, one point.

A *sumi-e* landscape and a portrait of Kannon, the Buddhist goddess of mercy, both painted by Onisaburo Deguchi. The creation of fine art depends on *aiki* integration between the artist and his or her conception, the artist and the medium, and the work of art and the viewer. Onisaburo said when he painted landscapes he lost himself among the mountains and valleys he was creating; when he painted a god or goddess he himself became that deity.

One of Onisaburo's fantastic "Scintillating Teabowls." In this case, Onisaburo did not imagine himself as a teabowl. Rather, he asked himself, "What kind of teabowl would the angels drink from? That is the kind of teabowl I want to make."

Ryu, the character for dragon, done in Onisaburo's inimitable style. He created this fabulous creature from just two big brushstrokes.

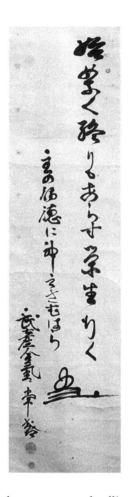

Master Ueshiba learned to love poetry and calligraphy from his guru Onisaburo and here is one of his *doka*, poems of the Way: *Hajime naku/owari mo arazu/sakae yuku/nushi no mitoku ni/kami no samuhara*. In English translation: "No beginning/And no end/But continuous glory./This is the august virtue of the Creator/And the benign protection of all the gods!" It is signed "Takemusu Aiki Tsunemori" (Tsunemori was one of Master Ueshiba's pen names). The large character near the bottom is Master Ueshiba's *kao*, his personal cipher. This poem was brushed in Hawaii during Master Ueshiba's visit there in 1961.

The literal meaning of the four large characters is "Open heaven, open earth!" (*Ten o hiraku chi o hiraku*) but it can be interpreted as "Unveil the mysteries of heaven, make your own path on earth." The calligraphy on the bottom says *iki no tamawaza* ("the spiritual techniques of life") referring to the opening of heaven and earth. To the left is the signature "Morihei." As we have mentioned often, "open" is a key word in Aikido.

(Top; read from the right) *Uchu o hitonomi*, "Swallow the universe in one gulp!" (Bottom) *Sankai aiki*, "Harmonize the three worlds!" Both are signed "Morihei." We do not think small in Aikido, and these two phrases are variations of Morihei's bold proclamation, "I am the universe!" That each of us is a miniature universe is the central tenet of both Tantra and Aikido. Morihei also taught that the three worlds of heaven, earth, and humankind, as well as those of past, present, and future are all contained in the eternal present.

(Top) *Masakatsu agatsu,* "True victory is self-victory!" (Bottom) *Katsu hayabi,* "Victory right here, right now!" Both are signed "Morihei." *Masakatsu agatsu katsu hayabi* was perhaps Master Ueshiba's favorite phrase, which he used to describe the essence of Aikido. The brushwork here is extraordinarily bold and dynamic, with a terrific zip to it that is truly inspiring.

Takemusu aiki brushed by Rinjiro Shirata. With *masakatsu agatsu katsu hayabi*, this was one of Master Ueshiba's favorite themes for calligraphy. *Takemusu aiki* is difficult to translate into English succinctly. *Take* is "martial," "chivalry," "bravery," "courage," "valor." *Musubi* has been discussed at length as meaning "creative life-force," so one possible translation would be "valorous, creative, and harmonious living!"

Aiki okami, "the great spirit of *aiki,*" brushed by the author. Aikido is a particular Path with its own traditions, philosophy, and techniques. *Aiki okami* is the universal spirit of Aikido that embraces all that we come into contact with during our existence.

Master Ueshiba standing, in a perfectly composed and natural posture, on a Noh stage. We can tell that he is a master, but if you did not know who he was what could you guess his art to be—Noh drama? Japanese chant? Tea ceremony? Calligraphy? Budo? All these arts have the effect of bringing out the best in human nature and making one appear noble and refined.

Aikido is a type of dance, albeit much more intense than a mere whirl around the floor. Here the Hindu deities Shiva and his spouse Parvati perform a dance that is both martial and marital. Shiva, who is known as "Lord of the Dance," wields a trident, the Tantric equivalent of the *aiki jo*, and a drum to mark the beat. Parvati moves in perfect harmony with her partner, the ideal state in both dancing and Aikido paired techniques. Even though this is a bronze statue, it is alive with *ki*.

Another kind of martial dance: two lovely women, clad in resplendent *kimono*, duel with a sword and a *naginata*. Although the female dancing instructors Master Ueshiba taught were not this fancily dressed, they were likely just as elegant and serious.

There are hundreds of photographs of Master Ueshiba performing amazing feats but, for me, this photograph says more about the man and about the philosophy of Aikido than shots of him throwing ten men at once. It was taken during one of Master Ueshiba's seminars in Honolulu. The master is in a corner of the mat, kindly and unaffectedly helping some befuddled novice with a technique. He is serving as her partner, and may well have taken a breakfall for her. (There is a wonderful video sequence of the master taking a breakfall for one of his child students.) Seeing photos like this reminds me of the Hasid who said: "I came here not to learn the profundities of the Torah nor to master the mysteries of the Kabbalah. I came here to watch the master tie his shoelaces."

Two candid shots of Morihei Ueshiba, martial artist supreme and Aikido philosopher, at age seventy-nine (above) and eighty-three (opposite).

Many Aikido students are professional artists and naturally they like to use Master Ueshiba as one of their prime subjects. This painting, "Master Morihei in *Misogi no jo* Meditation," is by Ernesto Lemke.

SUGGESTED READING

Deguchi, Kyotaro. *The Great Onisaburo Deguchi.* Tokyo: Aiki Journal, 1999.

Dobson, Terry, Rikki Moss, and Jan Watson. *It's a Lot Like Dancing.* Berkeley, CA: Frog, Ltd, 1994.

Merton, Thomas, *Gandhi on Non-Violence.* New York: New Directions Publishing, 1964.

Omori, Sogen and Katsujo Terayama. *Zen in the Art of Calligraphy.* London: Routledge and Kegan Paul, 1983.

Roob, Alexander. *Alchemy & Mysticism.* Koln, Germany: Taschen, 1997.

Stevens, John, under the Direction of Rinjiro Shirata. *Aikido: The Way of Harmony.* Boston: Shambhala Publications, 1984.

_____. *The Sword of No-Sword: The Life of the Master Warrior Tesshu.* Boston: Shambhala Publications, 1989.

_____. *The Essence of Aikido: Spiritual Teachings of Morihei Ueshiba.* Tokyo: Kodansha International, 1993.

_____. *Three Budo Masters: Kano, Funakoshi, Ueshiba.* Tokyo: Kodansha International, 1995.

_____. *Sacred Calligraphy of the East.* Third edition, revised and expanded. Boston: Shambhala Publications, 1995.

_____. *The Secrets of Aikido.* Boston: Shambhala Publications, 1995.

_____. *The Shambhala Guide to Aikido.* Boston: Shambhala Publications, 1996.

_____. *Invincible Warrior: A Pictorial Biography of Morihei Ueshiba, The Founder of Aikido.* Boston: Shambhala Publications, 1997.

_____. *The Cosmic Embrace: An Illustrated Guide to Sacred Sex.* Boston: Shambhala Publications, 1999.

_____, and Walthar V. Krenner. *Training with the Master: Lessons with Morihei Ueshiba, Founder of Aikido.* Boston: Shambhala Publications, 1999.

Ueshiba, Kisshomaru. *The Spirit of Aikido.* Tokyo: Kodansha International, 1985.

Ueshiba, Morihei. *Budo Renshu* (bilingual edition). Machida, Japan: Minato Research, 1978.

_____. *Budo, Teachings of the Founder of Aikido.* Tokyo: Kodansha International, 1991.

_____. *The Art of Peace.* Compiled and translated by John Stevens. Boston: Shambhala Publications, 1992.

PHOTO CREDITS